DRAGONS AND DIRT

The truth about changing the world – and the courage it requires

Commending you for the great job you are doing Hayes. With love & a commitment in Jesus & the Kingdom Pam

DALENE REYBURN

In loving memory of my grandmother, Doreen Grobler,
who struck the first match that would light my love for Jesus

I read the first chapter of A Brief History of Time *when Dad was still alive, and I got incredibly heavy boots about how relatively insignificant life is, and how, compared to the universe and compared to time, it didn't even matter if I existed at all. When Dad was tucking me in that night and we were talking about the book, I asked if he could think of a solution to that problem. 'Which problem?' 'The problem of how relatively insignificant we are.' He said, 'Well, what would happen if a plane dropped you in the middle of the Sahara Desert and you picked up a single grain of sand with tweezers and moved it one millimetre?' I said, 'I'd probably die of dehydration.' He said, 'Think about it.' I thought about it. 'I guess I would have moved a grain of sand.' 'Which would mean?' 'Which would mean I moved a grain of sand.' 'Which would mean you changed the Sahara.' 'So?' 'So? So the Sahara is a vast desert. And it has existed for millions of years. And you changed it!' 'That's true!' I said, sitting up. 'I changed the Sahara!' 'Which means?' he said. 'What? Tell me.' 'Well, I'm not talking about painting the* Mona Lisa *or curing cancer. I'm just talking about moving one grain of sand one millimetre.' 'Yeah?' 'If you hadn't done it, human history would have been one way ...' 'Uh-huh?' 'But you did do it, so ...?' I stood on the bed, pointed my fingers at the fake stars, and screamed, 'I changed the course of human history!'*

Jonathan Safran Foer, *Extremely Loud and Incredibly Close*

Foer, J. S., *Extremely Loud and Incredibly Close* (Boston: Houghton Mifflin Harcourt, 2005), 94.

Contents

Foreword

I have a sticker that clings to the window above my kitchen sink. I can see it even when the dishes are piled high and gritty with last night's dried-on pasta sauce that I really should have remembered to rinse before we went to bed. And when I stand in front of the sink, when I'm unloading the dishwasher, when I'm cleaning out yet another bottle of old milk, when I'm pouring water or fetching a clean fork, it's right there – the reminder:

'I am doing a great work and I cannot come down,' (Nehemiah 6:3, New American Standard Bible).

And now Dalene has written a book that shouts the message of that small sticker loud enough to drown out the days filled with doubt and confusion and last night's dishes.

However, it is not a safe book.

And it shouldn't be.

Because if we want to make a difference in this broken world of ours, we should expect opposition. Especially when it comes in disguise. Sometimes it looks like our own pride, our list of people who've hurt us, who owe us, our long records of old wrongs and brand new fears.

But for me, often it looks like that mountain of dirty dishes or unsorted socks piled high on the couch or the temper tantrums (sometimes my own) right before we're trying to get out the door. All these things can add up to me feeling small and incapable of changing anything in the world, let alone myself, my kids or the laundry that's been sitting in the washer for well over two days.

It's easier to believe that courage and calling look bigger, fancier than our Monday afternoon to-do lists. And that world changing looks like preachers and teachers, prophets and rock stars, bloggers, poets and politicians, all more qualified than those of us who come behind all bent over with our ordinary and embarrassed by our messy minivans.

We want heroes with grand lives to sweep us up into their stories and let us live vicariously through them as they change the world while we stay home and fold the boring laundry.

But what if we are the heroes we are waiting for?

What if we are called for such a time as this? Right here in the midst of carpooling and devastating diagnoses and planning toddler birthday parties?

What if we can change and mold and challenge and fight back the darkness from our own corner of the Kingdom?

What if ordinary is heroic?

What if we each stand firm on our portion of the wall and refuse to come down because we know that we are, in fact, doing a great work right where God has assigned us?

Dalene knows this. And her book reminds us all that most world changers wear jeans and t-shirts most days and fight fevers more than they make headlines. Most world changers don't have or care about blog platforms or their readership. They are too busy figuring out how to love their kids through a meltdown.

Most world changers are sitting right there in the pew behind us with their broken-down daughters, their aging parents, their newborns who won't sleep through the night, their prodigal teens, their singing off-key.

Most world changers are so ordinary we wouldn't give them a second glance in the checkout line. They reek of homework and figuring out the taxes and how to squeeze a date night into another crazy week of carpool and sports and getting one more stain out of the carpet.

Most world changers are brave because they keep going in the face of their overwhelming fears, their worries, the voices in their heads that tell them they aren't good enough, diligent enough, calm enough, prepared enough, or any other enough that can spit up out of the 'perfect-o-meter'.

Eight women I know spent a morning cooking food for the friend whose house was trashed by a hurricane, for the single parent who doesn't have enough, for the family who will likely knock on the church door tomorrow.

I have a friend who shared a photo of her toilet bowl and brush after a long weekend caring for sick kids and that photo is more powerful than any I've seen of her up on stage.

There is no showmanship in heroism. There is just the next thing. Sometimes that thing might feel small – like helping your kid with his Math homework. And sometimes it might feel big – like standing on a stage, or writing a book, or surviving couples counselling, or helping to build a school, or raising a million dollars to fight HIV/AIDS. But my guess is, heaven uses a very different measuring stick than we do.

So Dalene calls us to keep on at it – all of us who are up to our elbows in what feels like ordinary.

Her book and that tiny sticker above my kitchen sink remind me that all this – the kids and the chores and the grass that needs mowing and the friend who has hurt your feelings – all this is part of the great work that God has called us to do.

And while the great work I'm called to won't look the same as what you're called to, they will both likely require leaning into the small, daily acts of obedience and courage that – brick by brick – build a story of world change.

Lisa-Jo Baker

Mom to three very loud kids, social media manager to DaySpring, community manager for the millions of women who gather each year at www.incourage.me, and author of *Surprised by Motherhood: Everything I Never Expected about Being a Mom.*

A note to the reader

This book, it's my worship.

My act of obedience. My gift to God.

And, like worship often is, writing it was difficult and devastating and exhilarating and deeply satisfying.

When I sat down to write each day that it took me to weave these words, I prayed. I thanked God for the privilege: the time and space and potential to do this thing. I asked him for each sentence. I prayed for wisdom and life to flow from thoughts through fingers. I prayed, 'Jesus, let's do something beautiful.'

Disclaimer #1: Where I have shared an idea that someone else thought of first, I have given credit where credit is due. But if something I write is something you told me once and I have forgotten and it's been absorbed into my personal jumble of understanding and I've claimed it as my own, please forgive me.

Disclaimer #2: I wrote this book to honour God. I have shared parts of my story as I feel they reflect his glory, not mine. I have opened my heart, to open yours. And though I don't know how these words will land with you, I invite you into worship with me. I prayed for you too as I wrote. I am super excited to think that God might use my offering to do a great and lasting work in your life.

And, friend, this is a you-and-me-both book. This is a book which says that I've been there and done that but I *so* don't have the t-shirt. In Part 1, we'll brave the dragons that breathe fire at the borders of our influence. In Part 2, we'll dare to be honest about the dirt we hide in our hearts. In Part 3, we'll hold onto truths about the holy habits that slay dragons and scrub filth. And in Part 4, we'll get busy living – seeding our time and our potential into the lives of others. We'll do it together.

With love to you because he first loved us,
Dalene

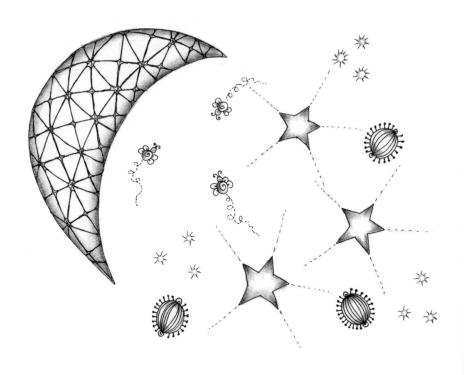

Prologue

Time, potential and changing the world

*Do all you can with what you have
in the time you have in the place you are.*

Nkosi Johnson, AIDS activist, b. 1989 d. 2001

*The way of the righteous is like the first gleam of dawn,
which shines ever brighter until the full light of day.*

Proverbs 4:18

Prologue

I used to teach English to high school boys. Sometimes I would ask a class, 'If you could have *any* superpower, what would you pick?' Because they were high school boys, their superpowers usually included planetary nuking and being irresistible to women.

My superpower of choice?

I want to change the world.

I want honest politicians. Untainted courtrooms. Superb schooling. Effective nature conservation. Accessible medical care. An end to rape and domestic violence and child abuse. Et cetera.

And yet societal evils are only the grotesque limbs of a sinister beast. Extremities keep on mutating if the heart pumps foul blood. So more than the righting of all these wrongs – and before that can ever be possible – I want the light of Christ to dawn across oceans and continents and in the hearts of people. Because changed hearts change behaviour – which changes society.

And I get that it starts with me. In the Hebraic tradition of reaching others for change and influence they say, 'One is obligatory. Two is a privilege.' I am the obligatory one. You are the privilege.

Because if *just I* can change, the world will be different. And if *just you* can change, the difference doubles and suddenly we're not just dreamers, we're revolutionaries and we're leaving the planet better than we found it.

So what stops us?

What holds us back from being the change? What hinders us from totally living? From filling up our numbered days of this magnificent, difficult life – earning our years – living them on purpose?

The truth is that there are external life pressures that punch our dreams in the gut. And there are internal heart entanglements that keep our potential buried deep. We look back with regret and we look forward with fear and we live a mediocre present.

Maybe, like me, you've always had a thing about time and potential and not wasting either of them. You want to decode the God-dreams

2

woven into your DNA because he has grown in you a passion for his glory. You want your one small slice of human history to reflect his splendour and if you get that right, one small slice will be enough.

But maybe, like me, you've lived things that make you long for the world to be different. You carry things in your heart that you wish you didn't have to. You get tired. And discouraged. And not taken seriously. Some days you dream dreams and close deals and some days you scrape last night's projectile vomit off the bunk beds. And, as someone has said, you allow the fear of not mattering much to keep you from what matters most.

Yet you have been uniquely crafted and gifted. There are things in you uncommon to any of the seven billion other people crowded on these continents. You have unique opportunities – a unique calling and a unique area of influence. Of course, the wonder that surrounds your life like so much stardust is there because God broke into darkness with blazing hope to call you Redeemed. Beloved. And all your wonder shines wondrous only when you know that you are not the main character of the story. When you live the wonder for his glory, not yours.

Throughout his ministry on Earth, Jesus pointed to an ideal – how people should live; how the world should work. Yet he never condemned those who fell short of it. Our success, then, in changing the world depends on shooting for perfect and walking in grace. It depends on a commitment to obedience that demands truth and courage. Because what needs to be done (truth) needs to be done (courage) and the doing is beautiful obedience. It will take courage to lean hard into truth, but these pages are about asking me and asking you to be honest. To be brave. To live fully – in the kitchen or the car or the boardroom or the bedroom. Because you and me – living fully – that's where change begins.

I hope you'll see that you can never change yourself. But you can build canals to channel the staggering floods of changing grace. I hope that you can find significance in the season you're in. I hope you will know, as you surrender to the Saviour your beauty and your brokenness, that you too have space and potential for Kingdom influence. And I do hope, for the glory of God and by his power, that we can change the world.

Part 1

Here be dragons

The truth about adversity - and
the courage you'll need to face it

There's danger before –
Danger behind – dragons wait –
God, open my eyes.

1

Rattled

It'll soon shake your windows and rattle your walls
— for the times, they are a-changin'.

Bob Dylan[1]

He never changes or casts a shifting shadow.

James 1:17b

Medieval explorers drew dragons on maps to show hazardous or uncharted territory. If there be dragons, you didn't be going there. If there be dragons, you didn't discover the splendour of new lands.

If there be dragons, you didn't change the world.

And I can see the dragons that have paced my borders. External pressures. Things I didn't ask for or expect. Things that life has thrown at me, to throw me. The dragons have hemmed me in. Hot breath withering dreams and diminishing influence. I know I need to hunt them down. But I'm too scared so they huff and drool and flick their tails. They feast on my time and my potential because I don't see the truth that dragons lose their fierceness – Gruffalo-style – when dragged from the shadows.

The first dragon – I smell its breath on the changing wind and that's how it gets to me and that's the name it goes by:

Change.

Because as much as I want a changed world, change can paralyse me. This dragon – shape-shifting unpredictable – it disappears and reappears and morphs into unrecognisable horror.

So I back into a cave, wasting my energy on fury. Or I run to anywhere but here and now. Or I stagnate into same-old-same-old.

I fight, take flight or freeze.

If I *choose* change, of course – like swapping my aisle seat for a window – then great. But adverse change – that I *don't choose* – is threatening. It's a force outside of me that can snuff my resolve to give my best self to the world because suddenly the world isn't what it was. And suddenly the calm assurance and confidence I had fostered around a set of circumstances falls away. I spend emotional and intellectual and spiritual resources recalibrating. It costs me time to adjust.

1.   Dylan, B., 'The Times They are a-Changin'', *The Times They Are a-Changin'* (New York: Columbia Studios, 1964).

Maybe you know this dragon?

Maybe you didn't actually vote for an economic recession and retrenchment. Maybe you didn't decide on a civil war or elect to be part of a displaced generation or opt for an autoimmune disease that would reshape your life irrevocably.

I live in a country that has gone through staggering change in the past two decades. Many of the changes – like the end of apartheid and the fact that my sons are part of a born-free generation – we've celebrated with wild dancing and the blast of vuvuzelas. Because welcome change is a reviving elixir that we drink deeply.

But some of the changes – like insidious corruption and a rising crime rate – have left us reeling from the fallout. Because change breeds fear. And fear lashes out in fight, flight or freeze.

In South Africa, some people fight with sullen stares and road rage and attitudes of entitlement and electric fences. Some take flight on Qantas or British Airways and then from suburban Sydney or Surrey continue the fear-speech-turned-hate-speech. Some freeze up – overwhelmed – because they think nothing they do can change anything because the necessary changes are too big and so nothing is precisely what they do.

I've been slapped with a few mild disillusionments, symptomatic of change. An attempted hijacking and housebreaking. An armed robbery in a restaurant. A cell phone nicked. That sort of thing.

But one night in 2006 stands out. A night when our family was too close to the epicentre of change.

No one phones after midnight with good news. From the dark of sleep and bliss Murray, my husband, went from zero to adrenaline before I could flick on the light –

'Dad.'

Silence. Disbelief. Desperate questions.

'Dad, we're coming.' We grabbed clothes. Drove fast and stunned through sleeping streets to the house he grew up in.

His parents, brother and sister had been drinking late-night tea – catching up at the end of a day. Three men walked in with guns and a terrifying agenda. They stayed for two hours. The family was hospitalised for shock and injuries inflicted by scissors and teeth.

It isn't our story to tell, but Murray and I would never be quite the same. Trauma is an emotional wound or shock creating significant, lasting psychological damage. When things break on the outside, things break on the inside. Core beliefs are knocked skew. In the months that followed that unthinkable night, I grieved. I grieved for my husband's family – forced to process harrowing memories. And I grieved for my country. I had to accept that it was different now. Things had changed.

So I've asked my questions and I've shaken my fists. I've been angry at the new normal and I've been angry at people who run away instead of staying to help. And then I've thought about running away too. I've even tried to subsist in a kind of cold indifference. I've mentally mined the shafts of fight, flight and freeze, but they're all dark dead-ends. None of them changes the world. I've tapped at their source where fear froths hot and irrational. And I've tunnelled deeper still and in the soul-pit, where things hurt and heal, the God-whisper is always the same:

Where is your hope?

If my hope is in this country or any other country or educational norms or effective policing or Nelson Mandela's legacy or an altered reality that I've learned to understand and love again – if my hope is in these things, the fear might shrink back a bit.

But probably it will fester and swell.

And return vicious.

And all these things I hook my hope on? They'll change too. Because wherever I live in the world, there's no sure hope in the certain flux of circumstances. And circumstances that shift and rock

12

can devastate me and I cower in fear. I shield my face from the dragon flames of change and block the changes I *really* want. Because the irony is that the severe effects of negative change can bar me from effecting positive change.

But if my hope is in a sovereign God who *never changes* – if my peace and my pace come from him and if I believe he is who he says he is and if I trust him to shepherd and shape my calling and the conditions of my life – then I'm less likely to be rattled. God speaks light and flings stars and multiplies cells and sets the foetal heart beating. He's way ahead of online cultures that morph and mushroom overnight. He's bigger than politics, bigger than physical safety or danger, bigger than what's trending today and forgotten tomorrow, bigger than both the landscape and the velocity of change.

He's bigger than fear.

But if change still has me dazed – insecure – ineffective: I read a book that never changes. I read of people throughout history who were confronted by change and became revolutionaries.

Like, a guy and his wife left their homeland not knowing where God was taking them. They built a nation. Another guy got that nation to follow him into a desert. God gave him a timeless covenant that has shaped cultures for millennia. A woman lost her husband and her home and followed her mom-in-law to strange territory. God gave her new love and a place in the lineage of Christ. Some friends watched their only hope bleed on a cross. God raised that hope. He filled those friends. He sent them. And they changed the world.[2]

So I'm thinking that maybe change is the catalyst.

Maybe unsolicited change at its scariest is handing me prodigious, unprecedented opportunities to effect the change I hope for. Strangely, the chaos of change can suck me into the eye of the storm where things are quiet. Perspective is distilled. Truth becomes clear.

---

2. Hebrews 11:8, Exodus 14–20, Ruth 1–4, Luke 23–24

I can resolve again to maximise my time. Search for what God has put inside me. Because changed circumstances demand that I find the courage and conviction to act.

I know there are changes to come. Blindsiding changes that will steal my keenness to make some changes. I know that in some parts of the world infrastructure will crumble and in other parts of the world castles will be built on complacency. But in every part of the world there is Jesus. Where lands and lives are decimated, he plants hope. Where change razes, he raises.

And I know that to slay this change dragon we need to stop our feeble fighting. Stop running. Stop hiding. Change doesn't take God by surprise. Inside time – outside time – all the time – he summons each new generation from the beginning of time.[3] He prepares beforehand the ground he wants us to plough.[4] He knows the physical and spiritual contours of the continent on which he places us long before he does the placing. He knows how the journey's terrain will change as we walk it. And he is the God who says:

> 'I will not in any way fail you nor give you up nor leave you without support. I will not, I will not, I will not in any degree leave you helpless nor forsake nor let you down or relax my hold on you! Assuredly not!'[5]

When the troops of Israel faced their enemies, the priest would address them before battle, saying:

> Listen to me, all you men of Israel! Do not be afraid as you go out to fight your enemies today! Do not lose heart or panic or tremble before them. For the Lord your God is going with you! He will fight for you against your enemies, and he will give you victory![6]

---

3. Isaiah 41:4
4. Ephesians 2:10
5. Hebrews 13:5, Amplified Bible
6. Deuteronomy 20:3–4

There's no quick fix for the fear roused by change. But as you wage war in your own heart – clinging to weapons of truth – there is One who fights with you, and for you. The battle against fear will not win you applause. But the life change will be undeniable. Time and energy spent floundering in the dark of anxiety can be channelled into world change. So I'm preaching to the mirror – that mediocrity isn't transformed into significance when the road is smooth. It's in calamity brought on by the mudslides of change that heroes – world changers – find the courage and clarity of vision to do the right thing in the right way at the right time.[7]

When the path falls away and changes erupt and the dragon belches fire? You and me, friend – we've got to keep our feet on the Rock that's impervious to tremors.

Because *I Am* still is.

---

7. An idea I gleaned from Andy Stanley's sermon series, *Heroes* (Alpharetta: North Point Resources, 2005).

2

Wounded

We can ignore even pleasure. But pain insists upon being attended to. God whispers to us in our pleasures, speaks in our conscience, but shouts in our pains: it is his megaphone to rouse a deaf world.

C.S. Lewis[1]

Here on Earth you will have many trials and sorrows. But take heart, because I have overcome the world.

John 16:33

I had seen the suffering dragon at a distance. Smelt the smoke when it spat fire on other people's lives. But the first time it breathed ugly in my face was when our eldest son, Cameron, was born blind.

When I look back on the days and weeks following Cam's diagnosis, they flash silent and disconnected like a slow-motion movie scene. People caught in an explosion. Screams but no soundtrack. Bodies smashed against glass. A shattering catching light.

Murray's father heart broke. I was numb with fear. We would have ripped out our own eyes if it would have made a difference to Cam. We couldn't understand why God, who loves our son even more than we do, wouldn't heal him. Our sweet tiny boy had done nothing to deserve this. And bloody hell, neither had we.

The prognosis was devastating. Cam endured batteries of blood tests and sonars and examinations under general anaesthetic. Each specialist had a different theory about the cause of the dense bilateral congenital cataracts and microphthalmia. Nothing was conclusive.

And Murray would have punched anyone who told him, 'Jesus wants you for a sunbeam.'

I had enjoyed a normal pregnancy and we had no reason – genetic or other – to expect a child with a physical disability.

The dragon had stalked us.

Swift ambush.

And suddenly, we were in the fray.

I felt shocked and unprepared. But when I looked down I saw that I was holding weapons. I hadn't noticed them because up to then I hadn't really needed them. Yet out of habit or instinct, I had kept them kind of polished. More-or-less sharp. God hadn't thrust me clumsy into combat with brand new equipment. Quietly and consistently – for years – he'd been supplying the weapons I would need to survive this battle.

---

1.   Lewis, C.S., *The problem of pain* (London: The Centenary Press, 1940), 82.

The weapons were all made of truth. But truth was more than my defence. It was also my doctor.

Because when this dragon's claws ripped open my heart, I had to find the courage to get truth salve into the bleeding mess of raw flesh no matter how much it hurt. Without truth, infection would fester.

As a student, I read and re-read Jerry Bridges' *Trusting God*.[2] It cemented my belief that God is perfect in power, wisdom and love. Which was hard to believe when we faced the trauma of Cam's condition. But because I had lived so long by this truth, it was my default. I *knew* somehow, still, that my God was almighty, all knowing, all loving. He wasn't cruel or capricious or too busy attending to the universe – back turned on me for nine months while my baby boy grew. It *couldn't* be so – no matter how much the dragon roared that God didn't love us, that he was punishing us, that it was my fault, or that this was just a random act of the universe. I kept up the mantra in my head: perfect in power, perfect in wisdom, perfect in love.

So when debates raged around us in whispers – did a loving God *allow* this or did a sovereign God *ordain* it? – I didn't need the answer. For me it was two sides of the same coin. And God didn't gamble. He hadn't flipped that coin flippant to see how it would land. Cameron's numbered days were all recorded before the first one dawned.[3] God hadn't taken his eyes off the eyes of my son. Not for a second.

I knew that 'Why do bad things happen to good people?' was the wrong question to ask. Because you and me and everyone? We're not good people. We have a debilitating congenital sin defect and anything short of immediate judgement is pure grace on borrowed time. When Adam fell, he took creation with him.[4] In this life we

---

2. Bridges, J., *Trusting God: Even when life hurts* (Bucks: Scripture Press Foundation, 1988), 93, 117 and 135.
3. Psalm 139
4. Genesis 3

can't shake off all the consequences of that cataclysm. The world is broken. Terrible things happen. Babies are born blind.

And it's not fair.

But it's true.

So the question to ask – resting and wrestling with the sure hope that God sees things we don't and will judge the world with fairness and righteousness when he rolls up all of history in his glory[5] – is not, 'Why?'

The question is, 'What now?'

I also knew that the answer to 'What now?' wasn't to be found in *Three Easy Steps to Becoming a Sunbeam*. I couldn't buy the answer on eBay.

The answer was: 'Start rock climbing.'

God's Word became my means of scaling the cliff up and out of the dragon's den. I found finger holds and toe hooks as I scrabbled sad and desperate from Genesis to Revelation. I stopped to rest in warm familiar hollows. Breathed the air and remembered the view from truths I had long loved. Gasped awestruck at old words made new because of where I found myself.

I hung on what Joseph said to his brothers – his betrayers: 'You intended to harm me, but God intended it all for good. He brought me to this position so I could save the lives of many people.'[6] Yes. That. It looks bad. But God brings good where it's impossible to see any.

I caught my breath in the Psalms.

When I was pregnant with Cam – before we knew anything about his eyes – friends had given us a baby name book. Each name in the book had a verse attached to it. The verse under 'Cameron' was Psalm 36:9: 'For you are the fountain of life, *the light by which we*

---

5.   Ephesians 1:10
6.   Genesis 50:20

see,' (emphasis mine). It was also the verse laminated and beautifully affixed to his cot at Heavenly Babies, the crèche where he spent his mornings from ten months old.

I wore Psalm 84:11 like a harness. It was my ultimate safety and stay on the cliffs – a life verse I had memorised when I was nineteen: 'For the Lord God is our sun and our shield. He gives us grace and glory. The Lord will withhold no good thing from those who do what is right.' Which meant that if Cameron having perfect vision was *good* for him or for us – good in the Kingdom sense, the more-like-Christ sense – then God would not have withheld it.

Because he will withhold no good thing.

No good thing.

And whether or not something *feels* good to me as it slips or sticks or stabs jagged in these hands – this *feeling* is not the flawless texture of eternity.

Murray still didn't want to be a sunbeam for Jesus or anyone else. Neither did I. But we knew this: 'The Lord will work out his plans for my life – for your faithful love, O Lord, endures forever. Don't abandon me, for you made me.'[7] God had plans for us. And he had plans for our son.

I camped on the narrow trails of Isaiah.

Cut by rugged rocks and feeling the sun on my back, I read,

'I will lead the blind by ways they have not known, along unfamiliar paths I will guide them; I will turn the darkness into light before them and make the rough places smooth. These are the things I will do; I will not forsake them.'[8]

I stared out at the night and Chapter 45 echoed across the velvet:

What sorrow awaits those who argue with their Creator.

7. Psalm 138:8
8. Isaiah 42:16, New International Version

Does a clay pot argue with its maker? Does the clay dispute with the one who shapes it, saying, 'Stop, you're doing it wrong!' Does the pot exclaim, 'How clumsy can you be?' How terrible it would be if a newborn baby said to its father, 'Why was I born?' or if it said to its mother, 'Why did you make me this way?' This is what the Lord says – the Holy One of Israel and your Creator: 'Do you question what I do for my children? Do you give me orders about the work of my hands? I am the one who made the earth and created people to live on it. With my hands I stretched out the heavens. All the stars are at my command.'[9]

I didn't totally get it. But I knew that the light from the stars I could see had been travelling towards me for hundreds of years and I knew it was true – that 'just as the heavens are higher than the earth, so my ways are higher than your ways and my thoughts higher than your thoughts.'[10]

Then again a few pages on – 'I will answer them before they even call to me. While they are still talking about their needs, I will go ahead and answer their prayers!'[11]

And I saw how the grace had begun to surface a decade earlier.

After high school, Murray did a degree in biochemistry and genetics. But it just didn't cling to him like destiny and he felt that God was calling him into optometry. He graduated, changed direction and started over. After four years, he qualified as top optometry student. Top contact lens student. Sexiest guy in the class. Everything.

A few days later, we got married.

A few years after that, Cameron was born.

We had to wait until he was five months old before it was safe to operate and remove the cataracts. His optic nerve would never

9.   Isaiah 45:9–12
10. Isaiah 55:9
11. Isaiah 65:24

recover from those months of being kept in the dark. A common misconception is that a cataract is an opaque sheet that can simply be peeled off the patient's lens. In fact, a cataract *is* an opaque or 'milky' lens. The patient's lens is removed with the cataract because they are the same thing. In almost all cases, a synthetic lens is implanted into the patient's eye once the cataract is removed. However, the surgeons couldn't insert intraocular silicone lenses into Cam's eyes because his eyes were underdeveloped. They had never seen a case like his. They said he had a fifty percent chance of developing glaucoma – increased pressure within the eyeball – which would lead to complete blindness within five years. They said he would never go to a mainstream school. Never read or drive. The causes were idiopathic, unknown, and they said we'd had a greater chance of winning the lottery.

Murray was the dad who knew too much. He wanted to fix things and take away our pain and the certain trials of the future, and he felt helpless. Everyone was saying how being an optometrist was such a blessing but, at the time, it felt like a cruel joke.

Yet in his brokenness, Murray began to see the miracles and slowly, with Cameron, he found a way through the darkness. Before Cam could sit, we began intensive visual and sensory therapy. He braved invasive ocular surgery. He wore contact lenses from six months old and later bifocal spectacles as well.

Compelled by grief and hope, Murray became a leading paediatric contact lens specialist almost overnight. He designed lenses that had never been made before. He would phone laboratories abroad and they would say, 'We can't make that lens. It's never been done.' And he would say, 'You're going to make it. It's for my son.' Today he helps so many families in similar situations. Cameron attends an extraordinary 'ordinary' school. He rides his bike. He navigates the classroom and the playground with remarkable intuition, an iPad and a sense of humour.

Because God answered.
Before we even called to him, God answered.

I climbed higher, through the gospels and the words of Christ:

> You parents – if your children ask for a loaf of bread, do you
> give them a stone instead? Or if they ask for a fish, do you
> give them a snake? Of course not! So if you sinful people
> know how to give good gifts to your children, how much
> more will your heavenly Father give good gifts to those who
> ask him.[12]

God hadn't ripped us off. He had promised us abundant life.[13]
And he proved that promise of life by laying down his own.

I found rhythm in Paul's letters. Holy arguments for grace and a
God who would cause all things to work together for our good and
his glory and would allow nothing to separate us from his love.[14] I
began to teach and write and live into the truth of 2 Corinthians
4:16–18:

> That is why we never give up. Though our bodies are dying,
> our spirits are being renewed every day. For our present
> troubles are small and won't last very long. Yet they produce
> for us a glory that vastly outweighs them and will last
> forever! So we don't look at the troubles we can see now;
> rather, we fix our gaze on things that cannot be seen. For
> the things we see now will soon be gone, but the things we
> cannot see will last forever.

When Paul wrote his letter to the Philippians from inside a
Roman prison, he had no idea how it would find its way to my
heart. But millennia later, God used the words to reassure me that
he wouldn't leave Murray in a prison of depression. He wouldn't

---

12. Matthew 7:9–11
13. John 10:10
14. Romans 8

leave me chained to disillusionment. I clung to the promise: 'And I am certain that God, who began the good work within you, will continue his work until it is finally finished on the day when Christ Jesus returns.'[15] God wasn't done.

And still, when we fear the future – when we wonder what life will look like for Cameron decades from now – we have this: 'I am the Alpha and the Omega – the Beginning and the End. To all who are thirsty I will give freely from the springs of the water of life.'[16]

God was there at the beginning. He will be there at the end. And always, he is life.

The truth is, pain got my attention.

When tragedy exploded in my life, it blew open my perspectives and priorities. I could see the things that had always preoccupied me for what they were: preoccupations. And suddenly I didn't care anymore who knew that most of my clothes were from Mr Price. It didn't matter if I wasn't tagged in trendy Facebook posts.

Like change, suffering was a catalyst that awakened something in me – a deeper urge and urgency to live fully. To invest my time and my potential in things that mattered more.

But my resolution around tragedy that required the greatest courage was the decision to keep on doing the Next Right Thing.

I started taking life five minutes at a time because five minutes was about all I could think about. And a whole lot of five minutes stacked up into days, weeks, years, and the momentum that built freed me, eventually, to find headspace for bigger decisions and long-term planning.

I didn't always get it right. Some days I was immobilised. I would lie on the floor next to Cameron's cot. Stare at the ceiling. Tears slipping silent. But courage every five minutes eventually made

15. Philippians 1:6
16. Revelation 21:6

for a lifestyle where I could again take advantage of the hours and opportunities in a day.

Murray and I have this penny-for-your-thoughts habit. At least once a day, one of us says to the other, 'What are your thoughts?' Answers range from, 'I was just thinking that we're nearly out of loo paper,' to, 'I was just thinking about the existential crisis faced by the slum-dwellers of Kibera.' Like, generally, there are thoughts.

But I remember one morning around the time of Cameron's cataract surgery. We were still living on the campus of St Alban's College, where I taught English. It was probably about 7:20 and I had a 7:30 class so I was standing at my dressing table putting on lipstick.

Murray said, 'What are your thoughts?'

I paused. 'I'm thinking about putting on lipstick.'

Not because I was a zombie. But because putting on lipstick was the Next Right Thing to do.

Next: grab laptop bag and classroom keys.

Next: goodbye kisses.

Next: walk out the door.

Next. Right. Thing.

Until another day was done. And then a few more days. And then years. And then we were through the worst of it and we'd developed a habit that boiled life right down to the instant. Reduced it to something rich and thick. Allowed us to taste the given moment. Because the given moment is all we ever really have.

Roman Emperor and philosopher, Marcus Aurelius, scribed this incredible wisdom, like, a very long time ago:

> Do not disturb yourself by picturing your life as a whole;
> do not assemble in your mind the many and varied troubles
> which have come to you in the past and will come again
> in the future, but ask yourself with regard to every present
> difficulty: 'What is there in this that is unbearable and

beyond endurance?' ... then remind yourself that it is not the future or what has passed that afflicts you, but always the present, and the power of this is much diminished if you take it in isolation and call your mind to task if it thinks that it cannot stand up to it, when taken on its own.[17]

So on really crappy days when I default to Next-Right-Thing survival mode, I catch myself asking, 'What is there in this that is unbearable and beyond endurance?'

This is the longest chapter in a book about changing the world. Because sideswiping suffering, more than most things, can hijack any good we're intent on.

For sure, you needn't look far to find people feeling the agony of this dragon's fangs. Someone who was raped. Who can't fall pregnant. Who was too young to lose his mom. Whose dad wasn't there to walk her down the aisle. Who shouldn't have been in that car on that night under the influence of those drugs. Who longs to meet a life partner. Who didn't deserve the blood transfusion that made her HIV-positive. Whose daughter should not have lost the fight to cancer. Whose son should not have committed suicide.

I know that you could probably fill in blanks I can't even conceive of and I rage with you against the dragon of your own heartbreaks. In *Walden*, Henry David Thoreau wrote, 'The mass of men lead lives of quiet desperation.'[18] Since having Cam, I've recognised all sorts of desperation in all sorts of people. Maybe your road has run out and you're on a precipice. Maybe you face a gradual but deceivingly long uphill and no one even knows how overwhelmed you feel or how you wake up each day wondering if you'll get to the end of it.

I pray that in the midst of your sadness or shock or catastrophe, God will galvanise you to shield yourself, with truth and courage,

---

17. Marcus Aurelius, *Meditations*, 170–180 CE, Book 8, #36.
18. Thoreau, H. D., *Walden* (Boston: Ticknor and Fields, 1854), 9.

from the dragon's enervating breath.

I pray that you will not be thrown into panic or paralysis, but that staring down the dragon will give you dauntless courage you didn't think was possible.

I pray that your pain will rise up in you as a battle cry for glory.

I pray that your brokenness will let the beauty of Christ spill from your life like sweet perfume.

I pray that the fragrance will fill the air, and change the world.

3

Exposed

It is not the critic who counts; not the man who points out how the strong man stumbles, or where the doer of deeds could have done them better. The credit belongs to the man who is actually in the arena, whose face is marred by dust and sweat and blood; who strives valiantly; who errs, who comes short again and again, because there is no effort without error and shortcoming; but who does actually strive to do the deeds; who knows great enthusiasms, the great devotions; who spends himself in a worthy cause; who at the best knows in the end the triumph of high achievement, and who at the worst, if he fails, at least fails while daring greatly, so that his place shall never be with those cold and timid souls who neither know victory nor defeat.

Theodore Roosevelt[1]

The Lord himself will fight for you. Just stay calm.

Exodus 14:14

There are dragons whose scales are jagged ice. They suck in warmth and leave the landscape frosted and airless. They stalk the temperate climes slavering for enthusiasm and optimism. They feast gluttonous on hope and passion.

Like change and suffering, the dragons of criticism, opposition and rejection can come at you in ways you can't control. They're fixed on having you believe that you don't have the scope to live significantly or to make the world a better place.

Their tactic can be small silent steps. Slow stealth. They may not crush all your hopes with a blow, the way change and tragedy sometimes do. They wear you down. Years of whispered lies. Trivial disappointments.

I am – and you are – the sum of all the acceptance and rejection we've received. And most of that acceptance and rejection happened when we were young – when our characters were supple and could bend to the weight that others placed on us, for better or worse.

I know a teenage boy who overheard his preschool teacher telling his mom that 'his lift doesn't go all the way to the top.' His lift goes way higher than that because, as little as he was, he understood the slur on his intellect and it has taken him the better part of fifteen years to walk free from the lie.

The effects of acceptance and rejection are not the same for everyone. We respond to these external influences according to our temperaments. Like, you can think of someone who blows off other people's opinions without a second thought, right? And someone else straining under extra luggage – marked 'fragile' – full of backhanded compliments and snide suggestions. We all have different contexts and different characters. But no matter your story, you're exposed to the elements of criticism, opposition and rejection. They're outside of you – acting upon you. If you haven't already, you will fall prey to them.

---

1. Roosevelt, T., 'Citizenship in a republic', 23 April 1910, transcript, Almanac of Theodore Roosevelt, http://www.theodore-roosevelt.com/trsorbonnespeech.html.

And the truth is that's not always a bad thing.

When I was heading up a high school English department, my mom used to remind me that if everyone liked me, I probably wasn't doing my job. If you want to be a difference maker, it's only a matter of time before you'll be the only person in a room who is really excited about an idea. You'll be the person on the receiving end of abrupt text messages *sans* happy emoticons. You'll hear the silence of indifference when you're hoping for feedback. You'll hear the reverberation of your dreams shot down.

To slay this dragon drooling the antidote for zest and spewing green-slime pessimism?

Do your thing anyway.

If anyone understood cold shoulders and hot accusations when his God heart was only ever mind-bending love, it was Jesus. And yet he never said it was OK to be pathetic. He never said it was OK to hide behind a victim mentality. He said get up and get over yourself and get busy loving the critics. Long ago on an open plain he said it hard-core to some people who didn't get it:

> But to you who are willing to listen, I say, love your enemies!
> Do good to those who hate you. Bless those who curse you.
> Pray for those who hurt you. If someone slaps you on one
> cheek, offer the other cheek also. If someone demands your
> coat, offer your shirt also. Give to anyone who asks; and when
> things are taken away from you, don't try to get them back.
> Do to others as you would like them to do to you.[2]

So here's the thing. You are probably not as important to some people as they are to you. Make them important anyway. Some people think your ideas are wild or stupid. Think of ideas anyway. Some of the moms pretend not to see you in the school car park. Smile and wave anyway. Some people don't text you back. Text them anyway.

2.   Luke 6:27–31

Sometimes you do all the inviting. Invite people anyway. Sometimes you'll make delicious food and your kids will say, 'Yuk!' Make delicious food anyway.

The sword of self-pity is heavy and blunt. I've chucked it. Because if I ask God to use me, then I shouldn't be indignant when I feel used. And if I say I don't do things for the thanks, then I shouldn't be piqued when thanks doesn't come.

Sometimes, the dragons only exist in my head. Some late Sunday nights and early Monday mornings they emerge from the trenches of my mind. They mock and scoff and leave me cringing exhausted before my weekly blog post goes live on Monday at 8:00 UTC+2 and my thoughts go far and wide and vulnerable to be trampled or ignored. And yes, it's ridiculous to feel criticised and rejected for writing that hasn't even been read yet. So I tell myself, 'Fix your thoughts on what is true.'[3] What's true is that every blog post I write, I write as an act of worship and obedience. What's true is that my editing criteria are truth, excellence and beauty. What's true is that I can't please everyone or control how a post is received. So I keep writing.

And where others are more relationally gung-ho, I'm prone to feeling easily spun out to the edges of the clique. I've learned that often this is a reaction that I choose in response to my perceptions, rather than the result of others' actual intentions.

But when I know for sure that I'm up against bitchiness or exclusivity or the obvious blizzard in the room, I take the weather with me. I keep the heart fires burning hot to melt the spite. Or I pray that God would strengthen me to skate right over the ice. And I pretend just a little. I pretend not to notice the aloofness. I keep smiling until I mean it. Because I know too well that succumbing to cold gusts of bitterness that rejection blows through the soul will wither my influence for Jesus.

---

3. Philippians 4:8

Exposed

***

I got my first teaching post when I was twenty-one years old and clueless. I made up everything as I went along. I still felt like I should call the other teachers Ma'am and Sir.

One Saturday, after a sports event at school, I was attacked by a parent. Not physically (unless you count the spit). I'm not sure if she confused me with someone else because her daughter had never been in one of my classes, but she spat (really) accusations about how I was always *staring* at her daughter and *judging* her and *discussing* her with other people and who the *hell* did I think I was and I had *no idea* what this girl had been through and to think that I called myself a *Christian!*

I was mortified. Just stood there. My mouth kept opening and closing. (Though I did try to keep it closed, because of the spit flying at me.) She went on and on, vitriolic. Up close and personal. I was absolutely intimidated. Hot with shock. When she finally left me alone, I headed straight for my car and dissolved.

I found out later that the girl in question had been raped. Almost certainly her mom was shattered and I had been hit by the shrapnel of her own devastation.

Still, I had to figure out what to do about overt criticism. I knew it wouldn't be the last time that this dragon would snarl flames in my face. I couldn't always run to my car for a good cry. I also knew that although the flames would scorch me sore, they would burn off the superfluous and I might see better the truth about me and what to do with it.

For some reason, I never expect criticism, whether nasty or constructive (and sometimes they're the same thing). It's not because I think everyone should agree with me. It's because I hate dishing it out. Even when people ask for it, I find offering criticism awkward and confrontational – and I assume that everyone feels like I do.

But when words slice and pride sticks in my throat I want to be

35

able to swallow. I want to get it graciously right, because the wisest guy ever said, 'If you listen to constructive criticism, you will be at home among the wise.'[4]

So I'm learning to take criticism like kings, prophets and poets.

Like King Solomon, who said, 'a gentle answer deflects anger.'[5] Deep breath. Quiet response: 'Thank you very much for sharing that perspective; I really appreciate it.' Calm retreat. Deep breath.

Like Jeremiah, who went to his toughest critic – the One who saw all his brilliance and all his filth and who told him,

> I knew you before I formed you in your mother's womb.
> Before you were born I set you apart and appointed you as my prophet to the nations ... Don't say, 'I'm too young,' for you must go wherever I send you and say whatever I tell you. And don't be afraid of the people, for I will be with you and will protect you.[6]

Like Isaiah, who kept talking because God said so. No matter how hard peoples' hearts were. No matter how few people listened.[7]

Like David, the sheep-watching baby brother of big brothers who didn't see him as the warrior poet and when they did see him, said things like, 'What are you doing around here anyway?'[8] David didn't allow them to deflate the passion of his purpose. He decided to be brave and vulnerable because the reward was great. He took on the giant, saying, 'You come to me with sword, spear, and javelin, but I come to you in the name of the Lord of Heaven's Armies – the God of the armies of Israel, whom you have defied.'[9]

And like Wordsworth, most celebrated of the Romantic poets, who said that poetry was the spontaneous overflow of powerful emotion

---

4. Proverbs 15:31
5. Proverbs 15:1
6. Jeremiah 1:5–8
7. Isaiah 6
8. 1 Samuel 17:28
9. 1 Samuel 17:45

recollected in tranquillity.[10] He'd go walking and then, 'Oh wow! Look at all those daffodils! I'm feeling so emotional right now!' He would go home, calm down, and write about it over a quiet cup of tea.

So I go home. Calm down. Recollect the emotion in tranquillity. Pray. Evaluate the origins of the criticism. Do the soul search. Ask myself the hard questions. Give myself the honest answers. And make tea.

Sometimes people are just mean.

Sometimes people love you enormously and want to help.

Either way, you can't predict all the criticism, opposition and rejection that you'll face. But if you have the courage to dream big you can be sure there will be naysayers. If you're resolved to live out your potential and be used by God as he chooses for his glory in a wrecked world, then be prepared to meet icy resistance.

The grace-laden irony is that criticism, opposition and rejection give you occasion to display the strength and the loveliness of Jesus. I pray that you will have the courage to look these dragons straight in the eye. Walk past them gentle and fearless. And find the clarity of vision to turn around and thank them.

---

10. Wordsworth, W., 1800, The Project Gutenberg ebook of *Lyrical Ballads, With Other Poems*, Vol. I., (emphasis mine).

4

Pressured

*Too many people spend money they earned
to buy things they don't want
to impress people that they don't like.*

Will Rogers[1]

*The Lord is for me, so I will have no fear.
What can mere people do to me?*

Psalm 118:6

There's a dragon that hisses about keeping up and giving in. It knows how to needle my ego and ignite my indulgence. The dragon murmurs at my neck – sweet-talking me with foul breath to believe I need to *feel* more and *have* more and *be* more.

John knew this dragon:

> For the world offers only a craving for physical pleasure, a craving for everything we see, and pride in our achievements and possessions. These are not from the Father, but are from this world.[2]

Pleasure. Possessions. Prestige.

Which are all good things. Good things from a good God because his plans are wondrous and mysterious and kind. He delights in us, for his glory. He gives us ice-cream and sex and satin skirts and long beaches at sunset and plane tickets and lucky parking spots and promotions.

But we can't escape the fact that pleasure, possessions and prestige can avalanche uncontrollably across the path of life. And surviving the avalanche demands a courageous response.

I'm an experience person more than a thing person. If I won an incredible prize and could choose between an immense shopping spree and an overseas trip, the overseas trip would win every time. So it's easy for me to get sucked into pleasure – pursuits that take time and emotion and intellectual energy and sometimes money. I fantasise about Facebooking sensational events because I know how the reactions will make me *feel*. I want to drink sublime cappuccinos and meet fascinating people and exhaust my adrenal glands.

The truth is that I *want* these things, so I'm willing to believe the dragon when it tells me I *need* these things.

And the truth is that if I want to change the world by living out

1.   Rogers, W., *The Quotable Will Rogers* (Layton: Gibbs Smith, 2005).
2.   1 John 2:16

the potential God has given me in the time he has fixed for my life, then I must find the courage to ask myself honestly – for every bridge swing and every slice of cake – 'Is this worship?' It could be worship. It *should* be worship. Because God created all the intensities of pleasure. And because reflective revelling – enjoying stuff and knowing it comes from God – glorifies him.

When our youngest, Scott, was potty training, unlimited Jelly Tots could not bribe him into doing a number two on the loo. So we launched Operation iPad. He could play games while seated on the great white throne for as long as it took him to produce the goods. It worked. Until he dropped the iPad on the bathroom tiles and the screen cracked.

Like I said, I'm not big on things. But I was mad. And the truth is I was madder about the dropped iPad than I was about the dropped fork at suppertime. Scott didn't know that iPads are expensive and that the ten-second rule doesn't fix a cracked screen the way it redeems a dropped fork. The misdemeanour was the same: a small mistake made by a small human still learning how to hold tight.

The incident revealed the truth that I don't always have my priorities straight when it comes to things. Which are, after all, just things. No matter how much they cost. Things given for our good – for our use and pleasure – but still just things.

In his book, *Don't Waste Your Life*, John Piper says it's good to work. It's better to work to have. It's best to work to have to *give*.[3] It takes wisdom to know the difference between stewardship and stinginess, the difference between generosity and thoughtlessness. And it takes courage not to clutch our possessions close. It takes courage to unfurl fingers that hold things in a frantic attempt to hold happiness. I sometimes picture balancing – carefully, responsibly, in open palms – all the things I own. I picture being aware that they

---

3.   Piper, J., *Don't Waste Your Life* (Wheaton: Crossway Books, 2003), 150.

could be taken from me at any time. I picture holding out my things for the God who owns the cattle on a thousand hills[4] because it reminds me that, really, my things weren't mine to begin with.

When I gave up my teaching career to pursue other dreams, like writing books and pretending to be an astronaut on the jungle gym, it was tough.

It wasn't just that we were one salary short at the end of the month (fewer pleasures and possessions). It wasn't just that I had stepped off the soft safe carpet of belonging in a career community (less prestige).

Beneath the obvious loss of job status there was a deeper loss of prestige tied up with what people thought of me.

I realised how much of my identity – my deep satisfaction that I was a worthwhile member of society – was fused with what I did. For a long time I'd been chasing results and measurable successes and the admiration and affirmation of my colleagues and students. Suddenly I felt quite bereft of value. Random call centre operators asking the simple question, 'What do you do?' got long explanations about how *even though* I'm *only* a stay-at-home mom, I *am* qualified as a *this* and I used to be a *that*.

I was uncomfortably aware of people in different corners of my life who were either dubious or supportive or intrigued or critical of what I was doing. I felt I had to explain and justify and placate.

And *please* them.

Which is entirely *not* what I said I believe – which is that my life is about pleasing God, not people.

A friend showed me that to slay this dragon, I had to follow the advice of John Michael Talbot.[5] I had to leave the cathedrals of grand ideas and go deep and daily into my cloistered heart. There,

---

4.   Psalm 50:10
5.   Talbot, J. M., *Hermitage* (New York: Crossroad, 1989).

I would remember that the truest thing about me is that I am the redeemed beloved of Christ. And from being loved flows my love for him. And from my love flows obedience. And obedience just asks, 'What next, Lord, to please *you*?'

I want to axe this pressure dragon because I don't want to waste my life chasing things and experiences and status instead of chasing my unique calling. And even chasing good stuff – like wanting to change the world – is not good enough. Because if my motive for chasing isn't to chase God – to follow hard after him – then anything else I chase, no matter how noble, adds up to idolatry. I'll miss wide-open opportunities to live bold and bright if I'm tunnel-visioned by pleasure, possessions and prestige. In whatever shape or form or handheld device they come.

Maybe you're not affected by stuff, titles and cool happenings. Maybe you don't think you're a chaser. It may still be worth scrutinising the subcutaneous motives that fire your life. Like, ask yourself this: would your identity or sense of worth change if there was a change – for better or worse – in what you wear or do or drive, in where you shop or live or study or travel or work, or in what others say about your ideas and decisions?

Or maybe this: what is it you talk about most? Where and how do you spend the most time and money? What motivates your outfit, your diet, your route to work, your calendar, your decision to emigrate or not, or the school you've chosen for your kids?

All these things make up the necessary stuff of life. But all this necessary stuff can switch insidiously into the object of our worship.

You'll know if you're pressured and chasing by the feeling of restless, relentless panic. The soul breathlessness. You'll chase because you want to *capture* – a thing or a position or another person's high opinion. When you start chasing, it feels sophisticated and cutting-edge. Then it just feels addictive and mandatory and scary. And then it makes you tired. And desperate. And mad.

Because you'll realise you're no longer the charioteer wielding the whip. You're the horse being flogged.

Want to know what I think?

Just. Stop.

Stop it. Stop chasing whatever you're chasing. The degree or the marriage partner or the skiing trip or the ministry or the compliment or the exclusive invitation or the cloth you're trying to cut bigger. The pressure of trying to please people – the ruthless carrot dangling of socioeconomic ambition – will leave you drained and disappointed. You'll retreat into a cave of inadequacy and fear, with the dragon smirking at the entrance.

And talk to God about it.

Pam Ferreira describes how sometimes you can feel like a Coke can at the bottom of the sea and the pressures of life are the deep waters getting deeper. Only God can maintain your internal pressure so that as external pressures increase, you can hold steady and strong without being crushed on the ocean floor. Ask him to help you recognise the pressure for what it is. Ask him to reveal your motives for chasing what you're chasing. Tell him how tough it is because of how badly you want it. Tell him that you want to *want* to stop chasing it. Then try to leave it with him.

Jesus knew this would be hard. That's why he said, 'Seek the Kingdom of God above all else, and live righteously, and he will give you everything you need.'[6] Which means it's not wrong to get excited about doing a PhD or walking the Inca Trail or dishing up seconds. Relish the good things God gives – the daily bread and the dessert – for his glory. But be aware that like all good things, they'll enslave you if you let them. Check your intentions before tucking into whatever is on your plate.

God has set you free. He wants to keep you that way. I pray that

---

6. Matthew 6:33

you won't let this dragon seize you. I pray that you won't be dragged to its lair and pressured to feast on things that will leave you hungry. I pray that you will find the courage to move only with the pressure to pursue Jesus. Single-minded sprinting for the Kingdom.

And the rest? He'll add it if you need it. Or leave it in the dust.

5

Overlooked

*We would worry less about what others think of us
if we realised how seldom they do.*

Ethel Barrett[1]

*For the Lord your God is living among you.
He is a mighty saviour.
He will take delight in you with gladness.
With his love, he will calm all your fears.
He will rejoice over you with joyful songs.*

Zephaniah 3:17

In 2003, I went to Canada to observe second-language teaching methodology in schools in Quebec City and Montreal. In one primary school, the teachers gave the kids an opportunity to ask the girl from Africa some questions. They were fascinated. Some of them were kind of awestruck. They wanted to know if I could eat with a knife and fork. They asked me where I got my clothes – as in, had I left my loin cloths at the airport and bought my jeans and sweater from duty free?

Those kids were great. No harm done. It made for a cool story to tell of how we all have preconceived ideas about everyone we meet, whether we mean to or not.

But sometimes misconception can be a dragon to slay.

This dragon is all about making us feel misunderstood and not taken seriously. Like the dragon of social pressure, it also pressures us to chase but its lures are more subtle. Acceptance. Affirmation. Affection. To be seen. To be heard. And like the other dragons – the external pressures of life – we can't control it. What people are determined to think of us (or not think of us) is their business. We can only try to understand how they are reading and interpreting us, and then manage our response.

It took me more than three decades to realise that not being taken seriously was a darkness draped heavy over my life.

I adored being the youngest of four daughters. But, growing up, being the youngest meant that I was the littlest. That didn't affect things within our family. Our parents treated us fairly to a fault. But to the general public – and to people whose opinions were gold to me – I was by default the least worthy of serious consideration. I was either teased, or disregarded, or thought to be simply adorable (and then disregarded).

I couldn't see it at the time but, looking back, I know that the

---

1.   Barrett, E., *Will the real phony please stand up?* (Ventura: Regal Books, 1972).

48

dread of not being taken seriously had less to do with pride (though for sure, my pride came into it) and more to do with deep insecurities that I had somehow gathered and guarded. Lies I had believed about not being good enough – or just, enough. So much of what I flung myself into was done to prove the world wrong. If I knew I had it in me to be the best at something, I didn't stop until I had done it – so that people would see and know and affirm.

I played netball right through my school years and loved it. But no matter how hard I trained and how high I jumped, I was too short and too un-athletic to play for a provincial team. But Dux Scholar? Now *that* I could do. So I studied. A lot. I remember once in high school my mom coming into my room and suggesting, a little worriedly, that I should come and watch a bit of TV. I sensed her unspoken, 'Or maybe, I dunno, get a life?'

And like, I couldn't do anything about the (un)prettiness of my face, but I had genetics on my side in the thin department, so for a while I worked impossibly hard at being as impossibly thin as I possibly could be. Because an impossibly thin girl is always taken seriously by boys. (I now have two kids and a slowing metabolism, so I'm totally over that.) The point is, my control freakishness went into overdrive in attempts to be noticed and given the OK.

It didn't stop when the teen angst simmered down. I poured myself into my studies and my career so that I always had something to add to the conversation. By the time I was twenty-five, I was reading for my Master's and heading up the French Department at the school where I was teaching. I owned property and I had a serious stamp collection going in my passport. I was also dating Murray and we were talking marriage. And one day I was introduced by someone who knew us both:

'This is Dee – Murray's little friend.'

Like, *what?*

I was properly grown up. Yet it seemed as if all that anyone would ever see me as was somebody's 'little friend'. I felt trapped in a changeless frame of identity.

Years later, over breakfast at Der Zuckerbäcker, a friend shared the God words that had risen up in her – what she felt God was saying – that there was a stronghold over my life and that it was this thing – This defeating, deflating fear of *not being taken seriously*.

There were tears. Floods of realisation as the waitress brought the bill and seasons of my life and singular moments and memories were sluiced crystal clear. It wasn't painful. There was just relief and release and a weird sadness and sudden understanding of so many things over so many years that had hurt. There was prayer. *Aha*. And peace.

Nothing on the outside of my life changed. But it didn't matter anymore who did or didn't *get* me because I was able to climb out from underneath the heaviness. Stand free and see how I'd believed I was always *less than*. And out here in the light with nothing stifling me dark and heavy, I could see the truth of who I was in Christ.

Many people still don't take me seriously. Even people close to me. And many never will. I accept – even embrace – that these people will only ever see the part of me that they can fit into a box of their own making. But the sting of being overlooked is gone. I can understand that, for the most part, people don't mean to be mean and for sure they don't know how their words and actions – or lack thereof – are going to affect me. These days, I have so much more grace for them.

And you're thinking, 'Um – aren't you taking yourself a little *too* seriously?'

That's the irony. I take myself a lot less seriously than I used to because I'm a lot less hung up on others taking me seriously.

It's like, I'm a nobody walking into a room full of somebodies. The King is there too. And he greets me. Calls me by name. Hugs me and asks me how I'm doing. Do I care if all the somebodies still think I'm a nobody? Abso-frikkin'-lutely not.

It's enough that God took me so very seriously that he wrote a cosmic love story and sent his Son to carry out the ultimate rescue operation on my life, paying the highest price in history to buy me back by taking on himself all the punishment that was rightfully mine. Not because he got anything out of the deal or because I was worth it. But because it was his good pleasure to impute worth, for his glory. He mapped my life from eternity past and Rubik's-cubed my DNA just so with my gifts and my glaring limitations.

He did all that for you too.

Around the time of the breakfast at Der Zuckerbäcker, I also began to see that anonymity – being overlooked or misunderstood or taken un-seriously – can be a gift. There's a transcendent freedom in being played down. It allows you to get busy doing what you're called to do because you're not waiting for somebody else's go-ahead nod. It's massively liberating to realise that your mandate is from the living God and you live your gifts brave by the authority he gives.

Of course, it makes for a far richer life if you get to share your gifts and live out your calling within community. But what if the community is overlooking the potential God has given you and the areas of influence in which he has positioned you? Don't let that stop you from doing what you do and doing it well.

I have a handful of inner circlers who understand me almost perfectly. But the truth is that none of us will ever be fully – wholly, ultimately – understood by anyone but God. None of us can climb completely inside another's skin and really – *really* – know what life feels like for them. Solomon wrote, 'Each heart knows its own bitterness, and no one else can fully share its joy.'[2]

You will be misunderstood. Guaranteed.

The King of kings – the One with whom you've had the courage to

---

2.   Proverbs 14:10

align your destiny – was misunderstood. So it shouldn't surprise you when people misunderstand your goals and dreams and priorities. It shouldn't surprise you when they think you're pathetic or paranoid, weird or wasting time, myopic and missing the big thing.

To change the world, you need to maximise your time and potential, right? So the enemy will do what he can to make you feel that your efforts are futile. He knows that if you're thinking, 'What's the point? They just don't get me,' you're likely to give up or give in or give over and abandon the truth you are doing or saying or believing because the misunderstanding of others makes you feel inadequate. The enemy knows that if you have been labelled 'substandard' and shelved, then it's hard for you to believe that you have something worthwhile to offer the Kingdom.

Andy Stanley makes the startling point[3] that only God gets to label you because only the manufacturer, owner or purchaser of something gets to stick a label on it. Only God made you. Only God bought you with his blood. You belong to only God. So if God has labelled you – and he has – joint heir with Christ, adopted by the King and clothed in royal robes for his glory – do you dare to argue with that?

When you understand the dazzling truth label that is stuck all over you, it won't matter so much how the dragons try to sear and brand you. It won't matter so much how you're perceived or whether you're appreciated. The serious certainty that Almighty God overlooks nothing – that he sees every thought and intention of your heart – will bring sure peace. Quiet confidence and constant courage. Delight, and lightness of being.

---

3. An idea from Andy Stanley's sermon series, *You'll be glad you did* (Alpharetta: North Point Resources, 2013).

Part 2

Dare to do in secret

The truth about your own heart –
and the courage you'll need
to examine it

None will see or know
Your wrestling in the wee hours
Wrestle anyway.

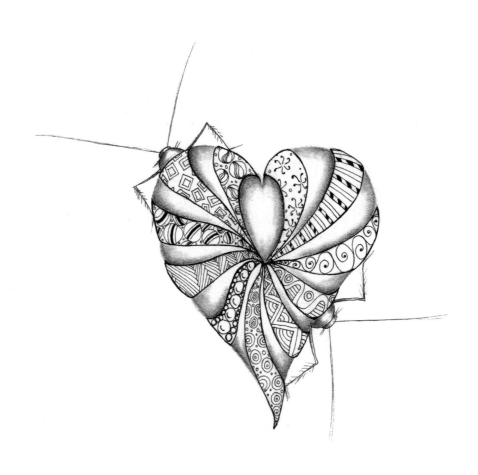

6

Marshmallows or cockroaches?

'Aaarghh! Cockroaches!' Toby hated cockroaches! They were running everywhere, even up his legs! He jumped about, trying to shake them off but kept trampling on more of them. Their gooey insides squished between his toes. 'Get me out of here!' he screamed.

From *The Adventures of Toby in the Land of Marshmallows and Cockroaches*, a Bugbox Animation[1]

Guard your heart above all else, for it determines the course of your life.

Proverbs 4:23

Last night at bedtime, I snuggled my Scott under his Pooh Bear duvet. He wrapped his arms tight and soft around my neck and asked, 'Mom, you got any cockroaches?'

One of Cam and Scott's favourite Christian kid animations is the one where Jesus shows six-year-old Toby that he has cockroaches in his heart because Toby is always fighting with his sister. And then Jesus shows Toby this cool love machine that sucks up cockroach goo and spits out marshmallows and Toby cleans out his heart so it's all sweet and delicious and then he cleans his sister's room and all is well.[2] So we've adopted the metaphor and I ask the boys when I kiss them goodnight or during quiet moments over Lego or toast: 'Any cockroaches? Marshmallows?' Lately, they're asking me too. Scott will say things like, 'Um, no cockroaches. Just Jesus.' Cam will say things like, 'Yes, I have a cockroach. I was frustrated at school 'cause Mike didn't want to play scuba-diver-scuba-diver. He wanted to play army-army.' We talk it over. Pray.

I ask my boys about their hearts because I want to know what they're hiding. Much more than that, I want *them* to know what they're hiding.

And that's what these next chapters are about. We've slain the dragons – the external pressures that stop us from using our time and our potential to change the world. But the truth is we don't have all that many enemies outside of ourselves.

It's easy to blame the dragons for keeping us from the spilling-over life Jesus promises[3] because we get to be the victims. It's easier to be a victim than to be a world changer. So we keep blaming the dragons.

For sure, the dragons lurk. But there's something more sinister than fire and fangs. Something more destructive than people or circumstances that beat us up unbidden. It's what happens on the

---

1. Argall, T. and C. *The Adventures of Toby in the Land of Marshmallows and Cockroaches*, DVD by Bugbox Animations and Yipee! Films (Durban: Integrity Media Africa, 2004).
2. Ibid.
3. John 10:10

inside of you and me that ultimately affects how we use our years, abilities and opportunities for the Kingdom. And because we want to live the full life – the best life, the God life – we need to be honest with ourselves and find the courage to deal with the dirt in our hearts because there's a link between moral purity and knowing God. It quite takes my breath away – what Jesus said:

'Blessed are the pure in heart, for they shall see God.'[4]

A couple of years ago, Murray and I felt that God was moving us to another church. Which might seem like a particularly small deal, but to us it was huge. We had been part of a tight community of friends and family for a long time and loyalties ran deep. Our church family had carried us through a bleak season – the first two years of Cameron's life. We didn't want anyone to feel that we weren't grateful for the prayer and encouragement, the food and friendship, and the significant common journey. We didn't want anyone to think that we were just moving on because something better had come up.

Still, the tug towards something fresh was undeniable. We needed to rest and recover from a season fraught with shock and grief, and the anonymity of a new community was a cool drink of water. We were drawn to different ministry opportunities and excited about a renewed spiritual vision for our family.

Call us crazy but we took about three years to make our decision. Part of the process was making sure that our motives were pure. That we were taking no baggage and leaving no unfinished business. That there would be no blowups or burnouts. Towards the end of that time of asking God to guide our thinking and decision making, we read Andy Stanley's book, *Enemies of the Heart*.[5] It was a life-changing teaching on how to check our hearts for dirt and get scrubbing.

---

4.   Matthew 5:8, English Standard Version
5.   Stanley, A., *Enemies of the Heart* (Colorado Springs: Multnomah Books, 2011), 11.

The process was difficult, intentional and liberating. God shone light on patches of my life that were damaged by guilt, anger, greed and jealousy. He humbled me by pointing out that the common denominator in all my relationships was, um, *me.*

Determined to make this move with a soft, clean heart that was right with God and the world, I started what I called The List Dare. I made lists. Pen-and-paper lists.

I'll get to all the lists in the next few chapters, but the first two lists I made were what Stanley calls the I-owe-you and the I-owe-me lists.

The I-owe-you list was a list of the people I had wronged. People I thought about with a twinge of guilt. Or a truckload of guilt. I prayed that God would bring people to mind and he did. An old varsity friend. An ex-boyfriend. That sort of thing. I wrote down the names. Then I made the call, sent the email, whatever seemed appropriate. I got in touch.

I quickly realised how much easier it is just to 'fess up privately to God. I had to be brave to own the hurt I had caused others. I asked their forgiveness. I didn't make excuses. I didn't mention the thing(s) they might have done to me. I just took full responsibility for my slice of the relational pie. And I reminded myself that I wasn't responsible for their reaction.

Here's an example: an email I sent to a friend (whose name is not really Sarah).

Dear Sarah

You'll probably think I'm totally weird for contacting you out of the blue like this! I know it's been a while. But God has been speaking to me about making absolutely sure that I have confessed and asked forgiveness for anything I've done to anyone I know, even in the fairly distant past. Murray and I have some big decisions to make, and we want to be sure that our hearts are completely right with the Lord and those in our lives, to be sure that we hear from him and can discern rightly ... if that makes sense!

I thought and thought ... and I asked God to show me if/where I needed to make things right. You kept coming to mind and, as awkward as this may seem, I just wanted to ask your forgiveness for anything I did or said to hurt or offend you in the years when we were close, and after that.

Looking back, I know that I was ungracious and insensitive. I know that our friendship cooled somewhat, hopefully mostly because you moved away. But I want to take responsibility for putting distance between us, even before then, and for any hurt or misunderstanding. Please forgive me.

Even though now I only see you on Facebook from time to time, I think you are a beautiful woman of God – inside and out. I've always greatly admired how you live out your faith. I hope for only good things, and God things, for you and your family. I'm grateful for the friendship and good times we shared way back when, and I trust that we can connect from time to time when we're in the same part of the country.

Much love and every blessing to you,

Dee

For me, it was super uncomfortable to make contact – in some cases after years – and then to ask forgiveness. But I was amazed at the grace that came my way. I was amazed at how gathering the guts to make myself vulnerable and risk all sorts of potential responses actually opened up pockets of understanding and reconnection and affirmation and *life*. Most of those I contacted seemed set free, too, in all sorts of ways.

From the I-owe-you list I moved on to the I-owe-me list, which asked: Where is greed clogging my arteries? Am I lying to myself about how much I deserve? When we have more month than money, do I doubt that God will provide for us? And when we have more

61

money than month, do we hoard fearfully? Spend hedonistically? Or do we say, 'God, what do you want us to do with your extra?' Do we *give* before we *save* before we *live*?

I do my best work when I've decluttered. I take toys back to the playroom. I close all the tabs and docs and apps that I can. And peace settles. Thoughts clear. Productivity soars. I do what needs doing when I've cleared the litter of life from my mind and my desk and the floor at my feet.

It's the same with my heart. And yours.

Friend, when it comes to your sin, kick ass and take names. Do a ruthless declutter. Be honest. Repent.

Because all the tarnished bits of you rendered useless under grime will suddenly gleam valuable. And because cleaning out your heart unleashes energy and stretches time. You'll use your best gifts and do your best loving and leave the best legacy if you've tidied up inside of you.

Take it from someone who's done it – and does it – and will need to do it tomorrow:

You won't regret starting a clean-heart habit.

Once you've operated industrial-strength degreasing equipment, it will be easier to wipe crumbs off the counter day by day. Because a once-off clean out is not enough. You can scour out the stuff that seeps foul from the past, but that doesn't make you immune to grunge that gathers every day. Dust settles and sticks and dirt attracts dirt. And cockroaches. You have to make heart scrubbing a no-arguments daily habit. Like brushing your teeth. Like, you'll feel gross all day if you haven't done it.

Of course, you won't win any prizes for cleaning out your heart. You won't get thousands of likes or retweets. No one will know that you have brought your dirt before the Holy God who knows it completely. And yet the most important things – the things of inestimable and eternal value – these are things done in secret for God alone because with no one looking on, you are your most honest. Your worship is truest. But the God who sees what is done in secret will reward you.[6] And there will be evidence in your life. An undeniable dawning of light and wholeness. A new peace and perspective. Greater good. More startling beauty.

Do you dare?

---

6. Matthew 6:4

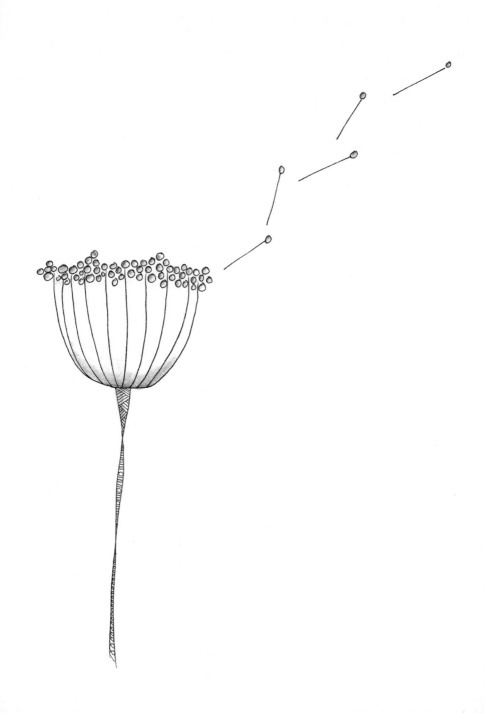

7

Free

*To forgive is to set a prisoner free
and discover that the prisoner was you.*

L. Smede[1]

*Get rid of all bitterness, rage, anger, harsh words, and
slander, as well as all types of evil behaviour.
Instead, be kind to each other, tender-hearted,
forgiving one another, just as God
through Christ has forgiven you.*

Ephesians 4:31–32

Freedom is the endeavour of life.

We fight for it from birth to death. Babies yell red to be free from the high chair at dinner. Kids skive to be free from school. Adults lie and manipulate to be free from responsibilities and poor-choice consequences. The ultimate civil punishment is to take someone's freedom of movement and choice. We want free rides and free time and free stuff.

And for sure when it comes to freedom, I'm like, 'Pick me!' I want to live free. And I want my kids to live free. Free to run and climb and shriek happy and learn and think and worship unashamed. Free to be all they were created to be.

But the truth is that we can give our kids the best, the freest, the fairest education and set them free to explore unthinkable opportunities and live in the freest and fairest and most benevolent of all democracies – and still they will never be free and they will never maximise their time and live out loud their astounding potential if their hearts are locked up behind anger, bitterness, resentment or hurt.

Because they won't ever be free if they don't ever forgive.

I realised that was true for me too. So after writing out my I-owe-you and I-owe-me lists, I made a you-owe-me list. The names on that list were the answers to: With whom am I angry? Who has taken something from me that they had no right to take – my lane in the traffic, my innocence or dignity? Who ignored my requests or ignored me entirely? Who disrespected me? Who purposefully left me out when they knew it would hurt me? *Whom do I need to forgive?*

I wrote down the names, if I knew them. From the neighbour playing loud metal at midnight to the teacher who humiliated me in Grade 5. I was honest with myself about the angry memoir I was writing in my head. This time, I did not call or email the people concerned. Those who had hurt me probably didn't know, and didn't

1.   Smede, L., *The art of forgiving* (Nashville: Moorings, 1996).

66

need to know. This was for me to take to God – to wrestle and sob out angry – and then to remember how much I had been forgiven – and then to pray, pray, pray.

Until I could forgive.

Breathe.

Say with lightness:

'I've cancelled the debt. They owe me nothing.'

'Like, *huh?*' you ask. '*How?*' Because I just said all that like it was easy. But how do you *really* get past the harm done or the time lost or the reputation damaged or the dignity stolen? How do you get past the rage?

I can only tell you what I did. And what I do. Because people keep hurting each other, right? You'll never reach some spiritual pinnacle and go, 'Awesome. I've done all the forgiving I'll ever need to do.' But you can get better at it – and quicker – with the practice that forms the habit that changes the heart.

I can also tell you that sometimes it's a long, stuck-on-repeat process of going back to God again and again and laying it all down – again – just to clutch it back close because it's just too hard to cancel the debt. But I keep up the rhythm of hitting repeat because the God who gives strength wouldn't have told me to forgive if it wasn't possible.

So, first, I **pray**. I tell God about the hurt or anger. And yes, he knows. He saw the whole thing. He even saw it coming. But I still unravel my stories in strings of words to the One who listens and loves and knows the nuances of every side to every story. I tell him what happened and how I feel about it. I tell him that I don't want to forgive the person but that I want to want to *want* to forgive. Kind of. Like the father of the boy with the evil spirit – how he cried out to Jesus, 'I do believe, but help me overcome my unbelief!'[2]

---

2.   Mark 9:24

Then I dredge up the difficult **Scriptures** – like the one that says 'Forgive others, and you will be forgiven.'[3] And I pray into and over and through those words until I start to feel them just a little – and find a way somehow to live them just a little.

Then I picture myself standing with the people whom I believe owe me something – like a big apology. And maybe flowers. And a tiara. I **picture the truth** that I am forgiven *much* and that all these other people have also been forgiven *much* and how if Jesus could look at them and say, 'It is finished,' then who am I to keep their sin on life support? Because most of these people, they're walking around in the world just fine. Light and free and unaware of my grudge. Oblivious to how I'm inducing a coma in my own heart and quietly dying.

And then, instead of watching the machines beep incessant when it's in my power to switch them off, I tell God that I'm pulling the plug. Clunk. It falls ugly-heavy from my heart. And I live into the idea that **I am free**. I've let go. No one owes me. I've released the offenders to the God of everywhere-all-the-time justice whose grace in my life has been so extraordinary that the thought of withholding it from someone else feels filthy.

But to forgive like this? You're going to have to be brave. Because if you're serious about cleaning out your heart, God will hold you to it.

After deliberately rifling through all the filing cabinets in my head, I thought my you-owe-me list was done. There was no one else I needed to forgive.

Some months went by.

Then one random Friday, all I could think about was the day that we found out about Cameron's cataracts.

I had taken him for his six-week check-up at the paediatrician. We'd suspected that he wasn't focusing – his pupils weren't dilating

---

3.   Luke 6:37

– and we knew for sure that he was extremely light sensitive. Our paediatrician sent me straight down the hall to an ophthalmologist, Dr Vermeulen (not his real name). He was the first of many specialists we consulted, but his consultation was by far the most traumatic.

I texted Murray from the waiting room to let him know what was going on, and I texted my mom, and my prayer group at St Alban's College.

Dr Vermeulen squeezed us in after ten excruciating minutes.

I didn't like anything about what happened next. I didn't like the way Dr Vermeulen's cream chinos kept touching my knees. I didn't like that he waved lights and peered and 'ummed' and 'aaahed' as I tried to keep Cameron calm on my lap. I didn't like that his assistant raised reprimanding eyebrows when Cam screamed as they pressed the sonar machine into his eye sockets and how she scolded me for not shoving in his dummy fast enough. Then Dr Vermeulen delivered to me the news that my impossibly beloved firstborn baby-powdered son had dense bilateral congenital cataracts and microphthalmia. And what I really didn't like was how he rolled his eyes when I burst into tears. The shock was flooding from my gut. Landing hot and dizzy in my cheeks. I asked him what it all meant – would everything be OK – and he told me condescendingly that I shouldn't overreact and put the cart before the horse.

Murray's car was in for a service that day so my mom drove to pick him up and they came as soon as they could. My mom waited outside. Murray conferred with Dr Vermeulen, who ignored me completely and told Murray in no uncertain optometric terms that the cart was already and irrevocably before the horse. There wasn't much hope.

Years later, I made my lists. And, like I said, I thought I was done. But that Friday, I couldn't get Dr Vermeulen out of my head. I had previously convinced myself that he hadn't meant to hurt or offend me. He was just doing his job. I was just another hysterical mother and I could hardly blame him for being a little desensitised when delivering a diagnosis. I *had* to rationalise all this because he regularly invited Murray to assist him with refractions for contact lenses during surgery.

But that day was different. The self-convincing wasn't working. God was needling me with the memories. And the feelings.

Anger.

I had buried it in order to cope and move on. But deep in the heart soil it had sent out roots of something a little too close to hatred. All through that day I struggled with emotional recalls and I knew I had to forgive. I had been carrying the fury – quiet and well behaved – for far too long.

I had arranged to drop the boys at my sister that night and I was meeting Murray at the mall after work for dinner and a movie. I parked and headed to Exclusive Books where he was already waiting for me. At the back. In the travel section. Talking to a friend he'd bumped into.

Dr Vermeulen.

No ways, God. Really? Like, now?

Murray introduced me – 'You remember my wife, Dalene?' Vermeulen's eyes met mine politely. A glimmer? I pretended brave and warm and small talked my way through five minutes that I don't remember because of the din of earth-moving equipment in my heart.

Dig. Loosen. Release.

Let him go.

Because it's true and I have to cling to it – what Richard Rohr[4] said – that if we don't transform our pain, we will transmit it.

And because finding the courage to forgive can change the

4.   Rohr, R., *On the threshold of transformation* (Chicago: Loyola Press, 2010), audiobook.

world. Forgiveness is our most powerful secret weapon for living full and free.

Do you dare?

8

Blinkers and
the better life

*It is in the character of very few men to honour without
envy a friend who has prospered.*

Aeschylus[1]

So if we have enough food and clothing, let us be content.

1 Timothy 6:8

'Mom, I sometimes feel as if other people have a better life than me.'

Cam says it into my hair from his pillow in the dark. It's bedtime when whisperings of hurts and happiness from a day lived loud come tumbling matter-of-fact as he burrows snug or kicks carefree at the curtains.[1]

It's been a squeezed-tight Saturday sandwiched frenetically between cricket matches and birthday parties and he has held it all together – brave – gung-ho – because it is what it is.

But now he's safe, and it all hangs out.

I keep my voice even. Speak slow and calm. About how fantastical he is at doing certain things that other people are un-fantastical at doing – which compensates, doesn't it? For the times when his world feels un-fantastical because the fun blurs past him too fast, too far. But I change my tack. He knows all that and tonight all that is not the point.

So I say something more like this: that the lie of the world is that we're missing out and that everyone else has a better life. That even as a grown-up I feel like that just about every day. But how I remind myself that God made us just so and placed us just here and set us on just this journey and loves us just unimaginably. And that these are our stories to tell – not the stories of another life that looks better or richer or fuller or more successful or more influential or more fun.

And there's more I need to tell him about all this. About comparison and discontent. And jealousy.

I want to tell him about another list that I scratched out 'til it hurt. The God-owes-me list.

This was the list of people whom God seemed to love more than he loved me. He had blessed them. Set them up for success of some sort. He hadn't done the same for me. And I was jealous. I felt like Job, moaning about how the wicked prosper and saying, 'So my

---

1. Aeschylus, *The Oresteia*, c. 525–456 BCE.

complaint is with God, not with people.'[2] I wasn't dissatisfied with my life. I was dissatisfied with God.

Like, I was jealous of other people's writing successes and social media followings and the acres of Kingdom ground they were ploughing. And I was going, 'What about me God? I could totally do that. Why aren't you making it happen?' There were – are – will be – always – people beating me at the game, outplaying me in one way or another. But it was especially hard to watch the success of others when I felt I was doing everything I knew to be right and still the big breaks weren't coming. And convincing myself that God was just suspending success to teach me a bunch of important stuff didn't really make it easier.

There were even whole groups of people that I resented. I was jealous of artsy-craftsy stay-at-home water-birth women and I was jealous of high-powered corporate-ladder-climbing Nine-West-heels-wearing women because I've never fitted into either group.

And I want to tell my Cam at bedtime that *all this jealousy is spawned by comparison.*

Because comparison constantly looks around at what God is doing for others – and it envies. Comparison forgets that, as someone has said, the Kingdom is a co-op, not a competition. Comparison steals your dreams. It punctures your confidence. It embezzles your energy and joy. It ruins relationships. It marshals minions of pressure and tension. You find yourself closing up, pretending, boasting, avoiding, seething, making stupid financial decisions and generally spewing the dirt of a dissatisfied heart.

My leaving full-time work a few years ago coincided with a friend's rapid rise in her company. As in, she bought it. Like a boss. She wore success beautifully – intoxicatingly – like expensive perfume. And I was driving my boys to swimming lessons and wracking my brain

---

2.   Job 21:4

for ways to make mincemeat more interesting and tapping out little blog posts that hardly anyone read.

I was jealous. I knew I had heart scrubbing to do. So I rolled up my sleeves and sunk my fists into suds of Scripture.

And I found that God's Word is littered with the debris of lives devastated by comparison. I'm talking real disasters. Saul compared his popularity to David's and then tried to kill him.[3] Jacob's less loved sons compared themselves to Joseph and then tried to kill him.[4] (A pattern much?) Sometimes the comparison catfight went both ways. Rachel compared herself to Leah (who was fertile). Leah compared herself to Rachel (who was hot).[5] The Pharisee compared himself to the tax guy.[6] Epic fail. Jesus' disciples were always jostling for favourite. He told them to get over themselves – to make themselves little, like kids.[7]

I saw the truth that comparing myself to others would make me either bitter or arrogant. Either way, not pretty. Like learning to forgive, dealing with jealousy would take courage and a lifelong commitment to keep on keeping on living the heart habit.

And yet it's *so* hard. It's so hard not to be jealous when someone gets what we want, especially when what we want is a good thing. Like a job that pays the bills. A baby. A break. How do we lay down those desires as sacrifices of trust?

As I reflected on my God-owes-me list, I started **praying**. I told God how messed up I was. How mad I was that he hadn't hooked me up with the life I thought I deserved.

Then I **celebrated** those people whom I envied. Celebrated their particular successes. Celebrated God's best for them, for his glory.

3.   1 Samuel 18
4.   Genesis 37
5.   Genesis 29–30
6.   Luke 18
7.   Mark 10

Thanked God for what he was doing for them or in them. I flung my joy, not my spite. I reminded myself that God didn't love them more than he loved me. I reminded myself that he has promised his best for me, too, and that I wouldn't want anything other than that.

Did I *feel* like celebrating? Hell, no. But I did. Outwardly and inwardly. I *decided* to celebrate. Forced it without being fake. Trusted that right feelings would follow as my heart caught up to my head.

I **stayed in my lane.** When pride rose selfish and cut-throat, I scraped together the courage to put on blinkers. I refused to look right or left. I remembered that this was my race and that no two races are the same. God has different Kingdom plans for different people. He has shaped each of us for his purposes. That's cause for celebration – and relief. I let the truth wash clean over me: you don't have to be anyone but you. That's why God made you *you.* There are you-shaped spaces that only you can fill. Get busy filling them. Paul writes to the Galatians, 'Pay careful attention to your own work, for then you will get the satisfaction of a job well done, and you won't need to compare yourself to anyone else.'[8]

I also realised that there was stuff going down in the lives of the people to whom I was comparing myself. I knew that I wouldn't necessarily like that stuff. Like mine, their lives weren't perfect. And Plato was right – we should be kind because every person we meet is fighting a hard battle.

I **gave thanks.** I made *eucharisteo* – thanksgiving – part of me. Ann Voskamp digs up the Greek roots of the word to show how in giving thanks for the grace – *charis* – we get to the essence – *chara* – joy.[9] Because thanking God is to jealousy what rock is to scissors. I thanked the Potter for how he made my jar of clay.[10] For how much he loves me. For where he has placed me. For the wealth of people

---

8.   Galatians 6:4
9.   Voskamp, A., *One Thousand Gifts* (Grand Rapids: Zondervan, 2010), 32–33.
10. Romans 9:20–21

filling my days. For opportunities to trust him in the face of others' strengths and my weaknesses. For the chance to be happy with those who are happy and to weep with those who weep.[11]

I followed Jesus. My friend, Samantha, reminded me that that's all we're expected to do. How, when Peter – miffed, glancing back at John – asked the resurrected Christ, 'What about him, Lord?', Jesus' words put him – put me – gently in place: 'If I want him to remain alive until I return, *what is that to you*? As for you, *follow me.*'[12]

And if we must? If we have to compare ourselves to someone? Let's make it Jesus. Because living brave for him, *like him*, will bring such deep peace and pleasure – such immense fulfilment – that it won't even occur to us to compare ourselves to friends, colleagues or anyone else. We'll enjoy these people like never before.

So at bedtime I pull the Lightning McQueen blanket snugger and tighter around us and I tell Cam that we need to be brave to beat comparison – to live the better life. But, I tell him, we don't need to be brave enough for the rest of our lives. We just need to be brave enough for the next decision. And after a Saturday like this – heavy with the challenges of a world beyond the rim of his vision – I want him to understand that not seeing the coach or the cricket ball doesn't make for a mediocre life. I want him to understand that the better life – the obedient, Next Right Thing life – is the wonder of arriving to play. The privilege of cheering for the superstar cricket kids because this is their thing. The fun of swiping wild and serendipitous and connecting bat to ball in occasional cosmic non-coincidences.

And the better life, I tell him, is leaving your case in the hands of God, who always judges righteously.[13] I want him to stop comparing – and see what happens. Because I know that when he moves

11. Romans 12:15
12. John 21:21–22, (emphasis mine)
13. 1 Peter 2:23

beyond the confines of comparison he will enter the promised land of contentment. And oh, the places he'll go!

You can go there too.

Do you dare?

9

Underneath it all

As long as you are proud you cannot know God.
A proud man is always looking down on things and
people; and, of course, as long as you are looking
down you cannot see something that is above you.

C. S. Lewis[1]

So humble yourselves under the mighty power of God,
and at the right time he will lift you up in honour.

1 Peter 5:6

The last dirt I need to scrape out is pride. It's last because it's deepest. Darkest. Nethermost. Bottom-line sin. It's the dirt underneath all the other dirt and it's where the cockroaches cling brazen and bombproof. It's last to be scrubbed because the truth about pride hurts most and demands the greatest courage.

And pride never bleaches clean forever. Sure, it was once-for-all nailed to the cross, but Earth-side I'm never going to say, 'D'you know, I have conquered pride? I am, like, completely humble.' Like all the other dirt I'm scrubbing, banishing pride takes habit, habit, habit. Keep spraying the sanitiser. And scrub, scrub, scrub.

Pride was the original sin, attributed to Lucifer who thought it would be awesome to play God.[2] It's the sin that mutates into every other sin because sin, however it manifests, always says,

'Me first.'

The irony is that Satan's me-first manoeuvres – his efforts at supremacy and pre-eminence – led instead to his disgrace. He knew he was going down and he tried to take the world with him. He hissed and promised the man and his wife into that first delicious capitulation in a garden full of life. Death was born. Death spread. Sometimes death streams and floods tragic. People die. Sometimes death oozes and trickles, insidious and imperceptible. Reputations die. Marriages die. Peace of mind dies. Trust and influence and opportunities die. But you can count on it. Pride gives birth to sin. And death follows. Every time.[3]

I cheerlead my boys. A lot. They bring me a scribble and I gush like it's the Mona Lisa. I encourage their every exploration into life because growing confidence in young men is crucial to the Kingdom.

But I would be doing them no favours if I didn't point out the destructive potency of pride left to ferment in their hearts. They

1. Lewis, C.S., *Mere Christianity* (London: Geoffrey Bles, 1952), 105.
2. Isaiah 14:12–18, Ezekiel 28:12–18, Revelation 12:1–13
3. Genesis 3, Romans 6:23

will never be all God designed them to be – for their good and his glory – if they spend their time hung up on themselves. Unaware of their need for a Redeemer. They'll burn up their potential trying to generate neon signs flashing kitsch 'me-me-me'. I want them to know how they're not designed to shine their own light but to mirror God's.

And I know my boys will have to tackle pride because they've got their mom's DNA.

Pride can drive and dominate my actions and attitudes. Like, I was the girl who didn't want to text anyone to say that I was safely home – and still stubborn – after a night out. And when Murray and I moved into a new place and my mom-in-law graciously offered to hem all the curtains in our house (which were dragging on the floor and gathering grime), I said no and very quickly did it myself. Some days, I hold imaginary press conferences in my head and I imagine that the BBC and CNN are fascinated by my opinions. At kids' birthday parties, I look down on the snobbery of the party mom whose surfeit of sweets and marzipan masterpieces cost more than a month of school fees. Yet it's never OK to enjoy feeling superior to someone else. Taking pride in being down-to-earth is pride nonetheless.

And, like I said, I can repent and be forgiven and know the assurance of eternal salvation. I can rest in the joy and relief of grace and God's goodness in justifying me for ultimate glorification in eternity. But between justification and glorification comes sanctification. Walking with Jesus in the now so that he rubs off on me. And I only need to walk a few steps with the Saviour before his fierce gentleness has me dealing with pride. Like, every day. After day. After courage-mustering day. Daily cleaning out my heart. Daily asking him to sharpen my conscience. Quicken my senses. Prod me. Love me. Humble me.

***

My battle with pride rages on, present continuous, and I keep fighting because 'pride leads to conflict'[4] and I'm all for soft hearts and harmony. So there are some things I do to kick pride in the teeth, since bad habits are defeated by good ones.

I start each day telling myself, **size counts**. When I dwell on how incomprehensibly brain-short-circuitingly big my God is, I don't even have to try to remember how infinitesimally crush-me-like-a-bug speck-of-dust small I am. If I can, I get out of the city to remind myself of this – even if only virtually. Climb high. Walk far. Dive deep. Read wide. The bigness of the world and humanity's probes into science and art help me to know I'm small. And yet this planet of heights and depths is an iota. A pale blue dot caught in a thin beam of light in a vast and boundless universe.[5] When I slow my thoughts on this, I no longer kid myself that God *needs* me. That he's so lucky to have me on his team. That he couldn't possibly spread his Kingdom without me. Um ... no.

But I need to keep doing this. Because I'm fickle and so quick to forget. Realisations that move me and humble me wear off and within minutes, never mind days, I've downsized God again – relegated him to bite-sized convenience – and supersized me and my agendas.

Next, I **forget humility**. Sometimes trying to be humble can feel a bit like looking for love. As in, you'll seldom find the man of your dreams when you're out looking for him. Mostly love hits you from behind – in like, a loving way – when you least expect it and definitely on the day you should have washed your hair. If I'm *trying* to be humble, then I keep checking on how I'm doing – as I would if I were trying to achieve anything – and if I'm checking my humility barometer, then the mercury invariably shoots up to arrogant.

---

4. Proverbs 13:10
5. The Pale Blue Dot is a photograph of planet Earth taken in 1990 by the Voyager 1 space probe from a record distance of about 6 billion kilometres from Earth, as part of the solar system Family Portrait series of images (http://en.wikipedia.org/wiki/Pale_Blue_Dot).

So I try to forget. Which is actually not as impossible as it sounds. My thoughts run quickly and easily away from me-me-me when I set them busily on you-you-you and God-God-God. It's hard to self-obsess or gloat when I'm getting my hands dirty for a cause bigger than me.

Another way I trick myself out of pride is to run desperate after wisdom. Because **wiser means lower.** I pray for wisdom because God promises to give it if I ask.[6] I look for it. Listen for it shouting in the streets.[7] Make notes on my phone. Memorise. Cup my hands around it and swallow it hot. Because the more I know, the more I know how little I know and I feel small again – a little person with a littler brain in the hands of an omniscient God. There's wisdom in God's Word and in common sense and in experiences brought into the light and understood. And wisdom says the world doesn't revolve around me because I'm a fleck in the wave of history that rolls on deep and wide and all for God's glory.

Lastly, I look up. At the stars.

Because I'd love to be a star. Not a rock star, but a twinkle-twinkle, diamond-in-the-sky star. I'd love to live a life *that* beautiful. I was so moved by Ann Voskamp's account of how she was looking up at the stars, so bright and so brilliant, and the thing that struck her was that **the stars are always small.**[8] No one is attracted to the person who is always trying to make himself or his life bigger. In fact, people who try to make themselves bigger? They end up looking shrivelled. Pitiable. Embarrassing. So I'm living desperately into the truth that it's in making myself small – going lower – passing on the glory because it's not mine to clutch and it's too holy to handle – that my

6. James 1:5
7. Proverbs 1:20
8. Voskamp, A., 'When it Feels like Everyone is Bigger, Better, Smarter [or 'How to be a Star']', *A Holy Experience* (blog), May 2014, http://www.aholyexperience.com/2014/05/when-it-feels-like-everyone-is-bigger-better-smarter-or-how-to-be-a-star/.

life becomes beautiful like the smell of cinnamon and the sound of waves crashing in the dark and a baby gripping my finger. And stars. I long to live, as someone has said, not so that my presence will be missed but rather to make Christ's presence known.

The world swaggers proud and spreads dirt about big living and small living. It tells us that we need a Big Life. Big name. Big bank account. Big office. Big ministry. Big boobs. But God is all about paradox. Using the weak to show he's strong. Going lower for greater glory.

My prayer for me and my prayer for you is that we would be brave enough to use our time and our potential to live small lives for the Big Name.

And bow low. Bow very low.

Do you dare?

Part 3

Sing it

Leaning brave into holy habits -
and the freedom that it brings

Choose my rhythm and
My rock: I'll live loud and bright –
The fragrance of You.

10

Rest

*Most of the things we need to be most fully alive
never come in busyness. They grow in rest.*

Mark Buchanan[1]

*Then Jesus said, 'Let's go off by ourselves
to a quiet place and rest awhile.'*

Mark 6:31

Before we rest, friend, rest in this:

You and I, we'll never be perfect.

Redeemed, yes. Even rehabilitated. But body-bound we're never completely free of the upshots of sin. Which means we will never use our time faultlessly or live into all our potential.

Jesus knew this and it blows my mind that he still appointed us to be world changers.[2] He gave us power through his Spirit to do the impossible and that power is perfected in our weakness.[3] I'm staggered to think that I might be used by God despite all the obvious gaps in me that need filling. And I'm amazed by how he fills those gaps with other people, and himself, so that my life – and yours and everyone's – can look like art.

So – in light of this courage-infusing truth – I'm thinking about what life would look like if we used our time wisely and fleshed out our potential in all the ways we know how. What if we embraced the unknown elements of life instead of fearing them and folding under the weight of them – not necessarily minimising the devastation but at least curtailing the debilitating shock? What if we were honest about the internal battles that we wage against sin and self – fighting ruthlessly for a clean heart?

Maybe we would begin to change the world.

Because if we can figure out the primary colours of character, which blend into the shades of relationship, which paint the landscapes of our lives – maybe we can change the colour of history. That's what the rest of this book is about.

But first?

Rest.

I wake up tired.

---

1. Buchanan, M., *The Rest of God* (Nashville: Thomas Nelson Inc., 2006).
2. Acts 1:8
3. 2 Corinthians 12:9

I surface through the dark into morning. Alarm. Fumble for phone. Kill it. Sigh. Lie. Lie longer. Legs over edge of bed. Feel for tracksuit pants, sweater, shoes. My sister, Mel, will be doing the same thing two blocks away so I have to do this thing.

We meet up in the cul-de-sac just before 5:00 and chat about all things serious and hilarious through cold streets just dawning.

Back home by 6:00, I reach for morning mugs because the world is better when there's coffee. And I think how today really started six hours ago when midnight ticked into the first unfilled seconds of an untried day, yet still there wasn't enough rest in those dark hours to recover from the life stuffed into yesterday. We stayed up talking way late and then I was wedged in Scott's bed between Eeyore and the wall because he needed snuggling at 2:00.

The voices in my head get louder with the lightening sky – shouting at me to get busy and busier if I want to change the world. But in the kitchen quiet of a new day, I'm strangely bolstered by the culturally counterintuitive truth that

Busy doesn't change anything.

Because if I want to live fully – taste life as I swallow it down slow – I need to be awake. Alert. And because work is a gift and rest is a gift – both given before the fall and called *good*.[4] Lived right, there's no guilt in either.

And I'm thinking it takes courage to rest in a world that's always telling us to go faster and push harder because it's a world that relegates rest into the shame-on-you categories of laziness or procrastination or distraction. For sure, I don't want to leak priceless time from the seams of a stitched-tight day because I'm stuck on a Pinterest board. I want to amplify moment by full bursting moment the hours I have so that they aren't frenetic – just *full*.

And rest is part of the *fullness*, surely?

Scott finds me in the kitchen. 'Mom I help you make coffee?' I

---

4.   Genesis 1 and 2

hoist him onto the counter so he can watch because kids learn what we model. Like, one of the first things God modelled for his children was rest: 'On the seventh day God had finished his work of creation, so he rested from all his work.'[5] He didn't *need* to rest. He wasn't tired after speaking out the universe. He was making a point. Declaring something holy. He commands that I rest and if I'm going to be an effective instrument of change in the hands of God, I had better obey.

And maybe, like it was in those genesis days, I should move from rest into work. *It was evening. And it was morning. The next day.* Maybe I should rest in preparation for work so that my rest is mindful – intentional – a laying down of me for the coming work of God. Rather than a collapsing – a petering out. Which is how it is most days.

I wait for the kettle to whistle steam onto windows and I realise that I generally see rest as a waste of time. Hours lost forever to sleep. Hours that I could have used for something constructive – like blogging at 3 a.m. Maybe I should start seeing rest as crucial if I'm serious about giving a good account of spending my time and my potential on God's glory. I need to learn how to rest well so that there is nothing in rest that whispers 'Slacker!' Whether it's sleep, or a slow stirring of Sunday soup, or sitting a little longer with feet in the pool – resting well should energise me and increase my capacity and effectiveness in terms of Kingdom influence.

We spoon ground coffee beans into the plunger and I wonder, 'Why, then, *don't* we rest?'

Because it's hard.

It takes discipline to put down the device and say no to distraction. It takes courage to argue with myself that I'm kidding no one saying that it's down-time when I know it's really waste-of-time. It takes brutal honesty to see the stuff crowding my life – my head space – vying for my attention and affection, and to own that Facebook is not

---

5. Genesis 2:2

a sin but unlimited indiscriminate addiction to Facebook? Maybe. It takes energy to simplify and find congruency in spreadsheets and schedules and supper menus so that I can build rest into days lived long and loud in this hectic, beautiful city.

The enemy fights for my time, my rest. He wants me to think I'm falling behind. I need to be brave to shut out the lie that busyness equals success. That I must – *must* – always carry the demeanour of being rushed and run off my feet. As in, 'Sigh. I'm such a martyr. And *so* productive!' I have to stop groping guilty for an airtight alibi when people ask me, 'So what do you *do* all day?'

The microwave pings the milk warm and I'm wondering how I can rest well so that I have strength and focus – emotional and physical energy – to do a few things exceptionally well and with purpose and intent. Rather than do three dozen things half-hearted, haphazard. I know already my boys will remember me rushing them into and out of the car every day. I do so want to stop the rush-sigh-hurry-hurry-eye-rolling. I want to listen and laugh and let them finish their sentences. Because at the end of my life it won't mean much if these boys turned men say, 'Wow, Mom got such a lot *done* every day!'

The coffee rests. And improves.

Scott asks, 'We going to Sunday School?' because he totally digs church and the chocolate biscuits he gets there. I tell him, no, because it's Tuesday. I love that the tug of the Sabbath anchors his week.

Sabbath. An old word for an old idea. Jeremiah pleaded with the people: 'This is what the Lord says: "Stop at the crossroads and look around. Ask for the old, godly way, and walk in it. Travel its path, and you will find rest for your souls."'[6]

Murray and I often ask ourselves, 'Are we the only people who feel *this* overwhelmed?' Because the feverishness of life can have us at the crossroads and caught in the headlights. Maybe we need to go back to old ideas, like: *Take a day off.*

---

6. Jeremiah 6:16

The idea wasn't old to the 24/7 slave nation of Israel – men, women and children who had been sweating under Egyptian whips, day-in-day-out of unending shifts, for as long as any of them could remember. Rest was a radical command. And like it was for those Israelites who couldn't believe there would be food on day seven even though they weren't working for it, rest is the ultimate act of faith. It's in resting that we *have* to trust God to provide.[7]

I can see how the Sabbath counters legalism and all forms of tick-box righteousness. The Sabbath says, 'Down tools. Stop trying so hard.'

The Sabbath is also common sense for finite creatures needing to be intermittently refuelled by food and sleep and hugs and eye contact and something hysterically funny. The Sabbath is a good habit – a beautiful, God-honouring thing. And though it doesn't have to be a sunset-to-sunset set time – because trains need to run on Sunday mornings and kids get high temperatures on Sunday nights – it's possible to isolate some sacred time to desist from checking emails and doing to-do's and filling up a day with obligation.

Maybe, this Sunday, I'll make space for inviting people to come rest with us despite the fact that we didn't make a single bed before leaving for church and the house is just our holy mess. Maybe I'll make space for contemplative tea on the *stoep*. Or ridiculous lawn wrestling. I will not make space in the rest for restless guilt.

Scott and I, we pour the coffee – settle rusks on saucers – and I give God the hours of this day. I give him our budget and our bank accounts. I give him my energy and ideas. I give him all my friendships and relationships and I ask him to play Tetris with my schedule so that there will be rest enough.

The day picks up speed and hurtles on but I find time to read and re-read the warning and the promise that come with rest. It's a big deal and all over Hebrews 3 and 4. There's rest and blessing for those who don't rebel.

7.   Exodus 1:13, 16:4–5, 20:8–11

Rest

Afternoon wanes mellow. Night falls. Teeth are brushed. Beds beckon. We snuggle close for stories and I feel full with the wondrous refuge of night when streets sleep and the planet spins slow to face out at a different part of the universe.

And I pray that as we rest God would whisper wisdom to us about the dragons and the dirt. I pray that dreams might be born in the quiet. I pray that as stars move across the sky towards a new day there would be new mercies. New possibilities for changing the world.

11

Christmas every day

The aim of life is to live, and to live means to be aware,
joyously, drunkenly, serenely, divinely aware.

Henry Miller[1]

Make thankfulness your sacrifice to God …

Psalm 50:14

Sing it

I'm all about the honesty so here it is:

I love Boney M.

I love their crazy Afros. I love their funky disco-era renditions of ancient holy carols. I love their proclamations of glory: *Oh my Lord, you sent your Son to save us, oh my Lord …*

I get it. I get that musically, Boney M is atrocious stuff. But it's my childhood. It's summer holidays and my sisters and me dancing on the lounge carpet in front of the Christmas tree. It's market shopping and tinsel and turkey. Scandalously, I have passed on this passion to my sons. Now, in March, and July, and every day from mid-October until Christmas, I get requests for 'Christmas songs pleeeeeez, Mommy!' They don't care that it's inappropriate – freaky – to listen to (bad) Christmas music in the middle of the year.

And I don't care either. Because of a trip I took in 2013.

Towards the end of 2012, while I was preparing to exit my teaching career, I read Ann Voskamp's *One Thousand Gifts*. It's her 'dare to live fully right where you are.'[2] And it totally inspired my theme for 2013: thanksgiving.

I decided to count 2013 gifts in 2013. It worked out to thirty-eight-point-something gifts per week, for fifty-two weeks. I blogged my gratitude lists, week in and week out of that year. No repeats. I kept lists in my journal, on my phone, on the fridge. Some weeks the thanksgiving was easy. I couldn't type fast enough all the blessings I saw and smelt, tasted and touched. And some weeks I stared at my screen and wracked my tired brain for scarce moments of joy. I learned how to give thanks even for very lousy things – because they were real and they had passed through the hands of God over my life and I knew they had purpose.

I didn't realise how much those lists and lists of things and things

---

1. Miller, H., *Tropic of Capricorn* (Paris: Obelisk Press, 1939).
2. Voskamp, A., *One Thousand Gifts* (Grand Rapids: Zondervan, 2010), subtitle and back cover blurb.

100

were changing me until I was done. By the time we headed down to the Western Cape for Christmas at the sea with my family, I had finished. I had said thank you 2013 times.

So I stopped.

Except that I didn't stop. I couldn't. I'd been searching so hard all year for goodness and the grit of glory that I'd forced a most beautiful habit. And forcing that habit of thanksgiving taught me to live in the moment.

I was looking for things that made me go, 'Thank you, God!' So I started seeing the way morning sun fell golden crisp on the wood of the dining room table – even though my two-year-old was simultaneously throwing a magnificent tantrum. If I hadn't been looking for the sun, I would only have seen the tantrum.

And that Christmas on the coast? It ranks as one of the best of my life.

The thanks habit had me seeing the gift – just the gift – of each moment – just that moment. I didn't drag baggage into every conversation, as I'm wont to do when the air is thick with the exquisite sadness of nostalgia. I didn't dredge up memories unless they were poignant – helpful – beautiful – to the moment at hand. I just lived the moment. And so instead of invoking the potential stress of Christmas, I let the wild flowers and the wet grass take my breath away. I listened to the ocean roaring praise and the Knysna turaco calling back. I watched my sons' Christmas morning exhilaration. Cam said, 'I'm overjoyed with all my presents!' like his heart would burst and I thought that mine would stop with joy and then I couldn't stop the tears when we sang 'Away in a manger' in the small hot wooden church with holiday strangers who smile kindly and greet warmly on a day like that.

With Ann, I realised that 'in giving thanks for the life [I] already had, [I] found the life [I'd] always wanted.'[3] Counting the gifts had

---

3.   Ibid.

made it Christmas every day. I didn't have to wait for once-a-year gifts under a bling tree. Because every day there are things to unwrap at the foot of the tree that split history in half – the tree that held the Messiah so we could be held by him in eternity, and in the here-and-now.

In 2011, *Time* magazine cited various studies proving that the optimism bias – the resilient belief that the future will be better than the past – drastically improves physical health and emotional well-being.[4] The truth about thanksgiving is that it's the heavy grace that tips the happiness scales. Thanksgiving keeps us from blaming others (or God or the government or the neighbour's cat). And that keeps us happier because blame is just another way of saying to the person or thing that we're blaming: 'Here! Take my happiness. Hold on to it.'

The courage that thanksgiving demands is to form a habit. Get a journal. Open a document. Be accountable to someone.

If you have kids, get them to start a thanksgiving habit too. A while ago, whining was fast becoming Cameron's regular and preferred medium of communication. It drove me wild. So every time he whined I would say, 'Come on, what are you grateful for? What happened at school today that was really fun?' We stuck up on the fridge a one-hundred-days-of-thanksgiving challenge. We would take turns at supper to say what we thanked God for. Three things a day. It took courage: discipline, effort and patience. And it took gentle encouragement because every night Scott wanted to give thanks for the tomato sauce, and for me, and I wanted to open his eyes to the wonder that there was *so much* more, so much all around him for which to give thanks. Now he'll call me back to their room after lights out in a state of great excitement: 'Mom! We forgot to say what we *grate* for!'

***

---

4.   Sharot, T., 'Optimism bias', *Time*, 28 May 2011, http://content.time.com/time/health/article/0,8599,2074067,00.html.

Some people, if you ask them, 'How are you?' they answer, 'God is good!' I always want to say, 'Yes. I know God is good. But how are *you?*' Because it feels like they're giving me a shiny happy cop-out and I want real.

But Paul writes, 'Be thankful in all circumstances, for this is God's will for you who belong to Christ Jesus.'[5] So is this Paul's vibe too? Suck it up and bloody well just say thank you? Should you be saying, 'Thank you, God, that I was abused as a child. Thank you that my car was stolen. Thank you for my postpartum psychosis. Thank you that I lost my job,'?

Paul says, 'in all circumstances'.

Jesus gave thanks the night he was betrayed.[6] He could taste the approaching agony. But in those dire circumstances, he didn't thank God for the betrayal. He thanked God for the bread.

Because there's always something – *something?* – to give thanks for. And even if you've scoured your circumstances for a glimmer of grace and found none – even if there is nothing left to be grateful for – God is in the circumstances and God hasn't changed. You can give thanks for that.

When we were wading through the grief of Cameron's visual diagnosis, I couldn't give thanks that my baby boy had been born blind. I could, however, give thanks for our family and friends who held up our arms when we couldn't anymore, and for the doctors and occupational therapists who dealt so gently with us and with Cam. I could thank God that Cam was such a sweet, easy baby. In time it became easier to thank God for his perfect plans, for his love, power and wisdom in our lives. It took some years but eventually I could move from sorrow to resignation to acceptance to embrace. To deep thanksgiving – the kind that thanked God for the whole journey, even the toughest parts. Because what I reaped in growth and grace

5.   1 Thessalonians 5:18
6.   1 Corinthians 11:23–25

from those years in the valley was irreplaceable. Priceless.

I sometimes wonder if Cam will ever be able to give thanks that his vision is what it is. I wish I could walk that part of his journey for him, but I can't. All I can do is pray the truth of God's Word over his life. And pray that he would find courage enough, to trust God enough, to lay down a sacrifice of thanksgiving. When Cameron was a baby, Murray had a dream in which he saw – heard – felt – a kind of prayer mantra that Cam was praying. We printed it in braille and it's still stuck on the inside of Cam's bedroom cupboard: 'Lord, help me to live in such a way that others wish they had eyes like mine.' I think often of that dream, and I give thanks, in faith.

Scott's favourite Boney M remix is 'Joy to the world'. It's a standard request, and he hums and mumbles it around the house some days. And I think how the truth is that always there can be joy because always there is the gift of the greatest story ever told: of a King born low to live astounding love beneath stars he flung. To die a promised death nailed to a tree he seeded. To rise so that we could be free.

Joy to the world – the Lord is come.

12

Four-part harmony

He who believes in God is not careful for the morrow,
but labours joyfully and with a great heart.
'For he giveth his beloved, as in sleep.'
They must work and watch, yet never be careful or anxious,
but commit all to him, and live in serene tranquillity;
with a quiet heart, as one who sleeps safely and quietly.

Martin Luther[1]

And you must love the Lord your God with all your heart,
all your soul, all your mind, and all your strength.

Mark 12:30

Sing it

It's an ordinary afternoon and we're dancing in the lounge because
there's music playing and I give in to the boys' wild request laughed
out dizzy – 'Spin me, Mommy! Spin me!'

We rock and reel and collapse on couches. I do it over and over
because music is a language we speak in this family. I do it because
I know something happens in the heart when we dance together
despite the pain and chaos of life. I do it because I want this family
to be a four-part harmony – yeah, very von Trapp, I know – each of
us singing our note close up against each other to make a common,
complex, beautiful resonance.

I work hard at the music we're making because the truth is that
Mom's the melody. I want to be the love lullaby – the soothing
soundtrack of my kids' lives. If I'm off pitch – too flat, too sharp – I
throw them off their notes too. It's noise. It's nasty.

But before I can harmonise I need to practise my pieces. Tune my
instruments alone with the Maestro. I need to find harmony in me,
with God.

I hear Moses' one clear note:

'Hear, O Israel! The Lord is our God, the Lord is *one!*'[2]

Before he splits the chord:

'And you must love the Lord your God with all your heart, all your
soul, and all your strength.' [3]

And the theme echoes and swells right through the gospels:

'You must love the Lord your God with all your heart, all your soul,
all your strength, and all your mind.' [4]

Heart. Soul. Strength. Mind.

So on this ordinary day, I'm wondering how to stretch my fingers
across the keys of twenty-four hours to play those four notes soft and

1.   Quoted in Rardon, J., '30 Lessons in 30 Days: A Handful of Tranquility', *Janell Rardon* (blog), 27 September 2009, http://www.janellrardon.com/2009/09/27/30-lessons-in-30-days-a-handful-of-tranquility/.
2.   Deuteronomy 6:4, New American Standard Bible, (emphasis mine)
3.   Deuteronomy 6:5
4.   Luke 10:27

strong and in sync with the Father. The piece needs to be played in the right key – the key in which it was written. Because that's the key to peace on the inside and the outside of life. The key to learning and living 'the unforced rhythms of grace.'[5]

And I'm aware on this ordinary day that time is a limited resource, steadily depleted at sixty seconds a minute. My heart has only so many beats programmed into it. Today I'm the oldest I've ever been. And I'll never again be as young as I am right now. What does God want me to do with all my age and experience? How can I channel my wisdom? What does he want me to do with all my youth and vitality? How can I channel my energy? Because there's 'only one life – 'twill soon be past; only what's done for Christ will last.'[6]

So I start hunting for space in every day to *love God.*

If I get nothing else done, I need to play the four love notes – heart, soul, strength, mind – and let the rest of frenetic life happen around them. I start practising the notes until they get gloriously stuck in my head – holy habits for harmony.

At the beginning of an ordinary day I make it my habit to feed my **soul**. I stay in the Word. Listen. Reflect and re-read. Maybe light a candle. Not to be weird but just because I want this to be time set apart and I want to be light in this house and on this planet.

Some days it's easy. Two psalms or a chapter of Luke or Colossians. Some days it's thick-sludge trudging through prophets and genealogies. But every day it's God breathed, I tell myself, and he wouldn't have put it in this book without good reason and I'll meet the King on these pages if I search.

I make loving God in the Word my urgent to-do. I find ways to keep it fresh. I find the plumb line that keeps me still and centred so that I can say, 'It is well with my soul.'

---

5. Matthew 11:28–30, The Message
6. Attributed to C.T. Studd, nineteenth century missionary to China and part of the famed Cambridge Seven.

Sing it

***

I find ways to love God with my **strength**. Because no one ever loved another someone without a body. This flesh and blood and the skin that holds it in – it's what I've been given to work with in my allotted time on Earth. It's what all my potential is stored in. I only get this one body to use for loving God and loving others. I need to do what I can to make it strong.

So I try not to trip on the skipping rope. I try to drink enough water. I try to choose unprocessed over processed. I try to ration the sugar. My boys are watching and I need to live a daily balance, not allowing the pendulum to swing idolatrous either way. I dare not make food or fitness, fat or fat-free, a god.

But the truth about loving God with our strength is that it takes courage and commitment.

In 2012, swimmer Michael Phelps was declared the greatest athlete of all time.[7] He said the way to win is to stay in the swimming pool. Stay in the pool when everyone else gets out. And when you feel like getting out? Stay in the pool just a little longer. Ann Voskamp comments on this:

> To stay focused when you'd love to be distracted. *To do the next thing when it's not the easiest thing* ... The most successful are the ones most focused and the greats are greatly focused. There is never any fruit without focus.[8]

I'm learning to stay at it – the practical, physical thing that keeps my flesh and blood fit and gives me the bonus by-product of greater emotional resilience and stronger, suppler reflections. I need to stay at the thing that I know will build my strength to love God and others. And

---

7. Joyner, J., 'Michael Phelps Breaks Olympic Medal Record; Greatest Olympian Ever?', *Outside the Beltway*, 31 July 2012, http://www.outsidethebeltway.com/ michael-phelps-breaks-olympic-medal-record-greatest-olympian-ever/.
8. Voskamp, A., 'How to Cultivate the Habit of Focus ... in an Age of Distraction', *A Holy Experience* (blog), September 2012, http://www.aholyexperience.com/2012/09/ how-to-cultivate-the-habit-of-focus-in-an-age-of-distraction/.

I need to stay at it for longer than I think I need to. Longer than I feel like. So long that I'll be wet and cold and tired. And maybe successful. Paul said it too:

> Don't you realise that in a race everyone runs, but only one person gets the prize? So run to win! All athletes are disciplined in their training. They do it to win a prize that will fade away, but we do it for an eternal prize. [9]

To love God with all my **mind** on an ordinary day, I stay on the wall. Like Nehemiah.

He had a thing to do. His secular vocation and connections gave him the skill set to unite and mobilise his people, spiritually and politically, against Persian opposition. The mission: rebuild the walls of Jerusalem. He was humble. He was just building a wall, not building a CV. He traded palatial influence for hard labour. He trusted that God was his promoter and he was excited about doing God's will for God's glory.

There were distractions because, as Jack Ferreira says, 'Destiny will always be contested.' Some guys who didn't like what Nehemiah was doing invited him for drinks in the nearby village. He knew they were out to get him. They didn't want him to finish the work. So he sent messengers to them saying, '*I am doing a great work and I cannot come down. Why should the work stop while I leave it and come down to you?*'[10]

My wall? It's the *main thing*. The thing that calls and compels me. The thing I know is God's thing for me in this season. The thing that's most easily and most often threatened by distractions.

So on an ordinary day I might say no to coffee with that friend and no to shopping for those boots and yes to banging out another paragraph or blog post or chapter. I say yes to reading wisdom and translating it into reality. I say yes to being the one to greet my boys

---

9.   1 Corinthians 9:24–25
10.   Nehemiah 6:3, New American Standard Bible, (emphasis mine)

at their classrooms. Yes to Lego. No to my inbox.

Because these things – they are my great work. I am *doing* it. I'm on the wall. And I cannot come down.

You and I, we don't have sinister Persians waiting in the shadows. Most of our distractions don't come with malicious intent and we needn't be aggressive in our refusals, as Nehemiah kind of had to be. Our interruptions are life happening. Dentist appointments and car services and long text conversations and online shopping and banking. Things that maybe we don't *have* to say yes to every time. Or things that can wait while we work on the wall.

And if people think your great work is inconsequential? Stay on the wall. Whatever your calling is where you find yourself – corporate ladder climbing or cookie baking – let your hands do the work of the moment. Live to the edge of your boundaries in the season you are in.

Loving God with all my **heart** on an ordinary day looks like forgetting about me. Being fully present to play, love, coach, cook, watch, talk, read, run and pray. To give all of me for all of those whom God scripts into my day.

I find it hard.

Because my phone flashes and beeps and the clickbait beckons and I need to manage all this before it manages me. I can easily miss the nuances of a real-life moment because I've got one foot on the ground and the other looking for traction in cyberspace. My inside life can be invaded by social media bullet sprays that splinter concentration and bleep out the Still Small Voice. And it's harder to hear other still small voices unpacking their days and their lunchboxes and their hearts while I pretend to listen and tap out another text. Jostling through the crowds in my head, I can find myself isolated – alone elsewhere – petit-mal absent from what's happening *now* – from those I should love *now*.

A study conducted by the British Institute of Psychiatry showed that to decrease your IQ by ten points in the moment you just have to check back into your email while busy with another creative task. The effect on your IQ is the same as going without sleep for thirty-six hours and more than double the effect of smoking weed.[11] I don't want my kids to have a mom who might as well roll a joint before signing off their homework.

So I try instead to *listen* because I will buy shares in their hearts if I pay attention. For their big dreams and mine to become big realities, I've got to slow into the very tick of this second. Forget my FOMO (fear of missing out). This is where it's at: right here now where God has me breathing. I'll arrive at the future in good time. And if I mess up by missing out on the now, it won't *be* the future I'm so feverishly imagining.

I can love God today by doing what today demands. I can live each moment so it bulges into the next making the minutes fat and full. Even the difficult minutes. Bend down, I tell myself. It's your highest calling. Look the little people in the eye. Weigh your words. Sit with them on the swing a little longer. Don't stress out trying to save time, then lose it forever because you've marred the minutes with hurry-up yelling. Giving people my undivided attention – listening to hearts – is never time wasted.

We could pray for our families, yes?

We could pray that, at the end of an ordinary day lived well, there would be no dissonance. We could pray that every chord would resolve to truth. We could pray for the courage to say no to stress and no to mediocrity. We could pray for the courage to say yes to an uncomplicated life – yes to the simplicity of loving with heart, soul, mind and strength – so that even when life's load gets heavier, the harmony of the music we're making would lend rhythm.

And, maybe, change the world.

---

11. Spencer, N., 'How to Destroy Your Productivity at Work', *Visual News*, 4 August 2012, http://www.visualnews.com/2012/08/04/how-to-destroy-your-productivity-at-work/.

13

Oxygen

*A man is what he is on his knees before God,
and nothing more.*

Robert Murray M'Cheyne[1]

Devote yourselves to prayer ...

Colossians 4:2

At seven months old, Mia Lotter was diagnosed with three hemangiomas – strawberry birthmarks – on the inside of her trachea. The largest was blocking eighty percent of her airway. Left undiagnosed for two weeks longer, Mia would have died. She needed nine operations and a tracheotomy. Her parents stayed up nights, taking turns to watch for every breath as she slept.

Numb with fear and fatigue, Joey, Mia's mom, kept calling and texting me to ask for prayer and to share small victories and to declare God's goodness throughout the long surgeries and critical recoveries in ICU.

Then one night, both of Mia's lungs collapsed. Because of her small size and critical condition, the medical team was having trouble with her tracheotomy, which kept falling out or closing up. They rushed her into theatre. The normally forty-five-minute procedure turned into two hours. Joey walked outside to phone me and our mutual friend, Tracy. She stood by the rose bushes at the entrance of the Zuid-Afrikaans Hospital in Bourke Street, Pretoria, and her heart broke. She told us it was time to pray. Really pray. Then she told God that if he had to take her daughter that night – well, fine. But that she thought it was pretty unfair because she'd hardly had time to get to know her.

There were hundreds – maybe thousands – of people praying for Mia. But it was me and Tracy whom Joey called that night. She said she just knew we needed to pray. We weren't better equipped than anyone else. We didn't have a special dispensation. Our voices weren't louder. But for some reason, praying for Mia was our special assignment that night.

So I lay wide awake through dark hours. Arrested by a desperate urgency to plead with God for this baby girl's life. A few blocks away, Tracy was going through the same thing. I kept thinking of

---

1. Quoted in The Robert Murray M'Cheyne Resource, http://www.mcheyne.info/quotes.php

Jacob's hip-dislocating wrestle with God.[2] My hips were fine the next morning but I felt like I'd been smacked by a bus. I knew – like how you just know that you know – that I'd been part of something much, much bigger than me. Something that had lasted all night. Something that demanded my physical strength and every thread of my spiritual being. I don't understand exactly what happened. I don't know how or why God used my prayers or Tracy's or anyone else's. But Mia made it through the night – turned a corner – and started recovering.

There was another night, years before, in Mozambique. We were students on a short-term mission trip, doing outreaches to women and children in rural villages and showing the Jesus Film against the walls of crumbling buildings in Maputo. While the film played, the team took turns to pray in pairs for half an hour at a time. So my friend, Shirley, and I did our shift in the minivan we were using for transport. I remember that half hour as another one of the times I've felt the power of prayer to shift things in the physical and spiritual domain. It felt like a couple of minutes. I didn't want it to be over. And that night floods of people accepted Jesus.

Experiences like that leave me awestruck – humbled – super excited about this thing called prayer. But then there are times when prayer feels futile. Unheard.

I've prayed for people's salvation for *years*: no change. And I know for a fact that people on every continent prayed for Cameron's healing when he was diagnosed blind. He wasn't healed. Murray still prays often and earnestly for God to heal Cam completely. His prayer is always for God's glory. That God would do something miraculous – that Cam's healing would be a story to tell of God's goodness and magnificence. God hasn't answered – doesn't or won't answer? – that prayer.

---

2. Genesis 32

When I'm faced with the encouraging and discouraging complexities around answered and unanswered prayer, it helps to go back to truth and courage. Because the truth is that we are commanded to pray. Courageously.[3]

My experience has been that God calls us to pray differently in different seasons. There are different kinds of prayer. Different ways of praying. Sometimes you have an unmistakeable appointment to pray into another realm in the back of a minivan in Maputo. Sometimes you multitask pray, eyes wide open in the midst of a tough conversation. My friend, Lauren, is deeply compelled to pray for marriages. I have a burden to pray for the police force of South Africa. You might have a heart to pray into some other cause, like kids' ministry or people's financial struggles or single parents or the leaders in your city.

It's true that prayer can be awkward. Public prayer takes courage: the closing of eyes to address an unseen presence in a sceptical, concrete world. The first time someone prayed for me in a coffee shop – a busy coffee shop in which there were other people drinking coffee, not praying – I cringed just a bit. Then I thought about how the opinion of the coffee drinkers wouldn't mean much to me in eternity. Indeed, the opinion of the coffee drinkers didn't mean much on that day either.

It's true that every denomination and subculture of Christianity has different semantics, different buzz words and habits and favourite expressions of prayer. I've been part of Methodist and Anglican congregations and I love muttering low and reverent, head bowed in wooden pews,

> We do not presume
> to come to this your table, merciful Lord,
> trusting in our own righteousness,
> but in your manifold and great mercies …

---

3.   Colossians 4:2–4, Ephesians 6:18–19

And I've been part of reformed evangelical, Baptist and charismatic congregations, and I love hands lifted high and unashamed in honest say-it-like-it-is prayer:

Father we just come to you today and we …

Because God sees the heart of every person who prays and that humbles me. Anyone in any context can put on a show. And anyone in any context can pour themselves out unaffected in the deep, otherworldly language of prayer. How the words are rehearsed or stumbled out honest and raw – this is not for me to judge.

What I *am* responsible for? The courage to step out in faith and pray enormous prayers. The kind of prayers where if God doesn't come through for me? I'm screwed. Because if I pray for nothing then for sure I'll get no answer. And safe prayers that don't leave room for doubt and hope and putting all my money on God – those prayers don't change the world.

We pray with our boys in the car. In the kitchen. At bedtime. Whenever we feel the nudge. In traffic on the way to school, we commit the day to God. We pray that he would protect their hearts and fill them with peace, joy and a sense of his presence and love for them. That he would bless them to be a blessing to others. I guess they pick up on what, when and how we pray. One Sunday night Cam prayed earnest from his pillow for the week ahead. He said, 'Jesus, please give us wisdom, strength and descendants.' A post-prayer debrief ensued. I discerned (ha!) that discernment was what he had meant.

At night, if I can stay awake, Murray and I pray together. It quiets me and gives me hope that we might just survive all the crazy because we're in the hands of a very big God.

But the greatest courage that prayer demands of me is to make it my oxygen. The life breathed into my existence. Daily, present continuous, quiet breath prayers. Because no one sees or knows about those prayers. And maybe no one will even see or know about their effects. But I thrill to imagine every believer on every patch of this rock revolving around the sun walking through their days murmuring, thinking, sighing out one-liners to the King as they sign deals and homework diaries and as they drop kids at school and seeds into earth. Because *those* kinds of prayers whispered out of our ordinary are, paradoxically, never as small as they seem. Those kinds of prayers can change the world.

I have a morning mantra to start my days: 'Jesus, from beginning to end of this day …'. And then I pray backwards from bedtime to breakfast.

First, I picture kissing Murray goodnight and switching off my lamp – because I want the last awake moments of this day to be good – maybe even magical. Then I reverse, picturing all the things planned for the day. The balls I'll kick across the lawn and the snacks I'll slice and spread. The people I'll see and interact with. The conversations and the workload and the lousy obligations and the stuff I'm really excited about. I pray for words of life and wisdom. For guidance and discernment and for the things I don't have planned but that God does – that I would leave margins in the day for unscheduled events to be penned in by the One to whom I've submitted my time.

One of my friends and mentors, Sheyne, lives the holy habit of reading Scripture in the morning and then dwelling on it every time she switches on the kettle for the rest of the day. The Word doesn't just fly in and out of her consciousness. A few times a day she brings it to mind – savours it. And because I need help to stay focused, I have set up all sorts of prayer reminders like that.

When I'm straightening my hair – 'Oh God, make my paths straight.'

When I'm undertaking the impossible task of looking for a matching lunchbox lid in the Tupperware drawer, I redeem the time wasted – 'God, give Murray extraordinary wisdom today with every patient he sees. Grant him favour. Give him integrity and courage and clarity of thought.'

When I open the curtains in the morning – 'Lord, please open our hearts. Open our home to those who need refuge or comfort.'

When I switch on or off the outside security lights around the house – 'God, help us not to try to shine our own light but only to reflect yours.'

When I water the coral creeper I'm growing on the kitchen window sill – 'Jesus, make this family like a well-watered garden.'

When I drive to an appointment or when I sit down at my laptop or when I set the table for a dinner party – 'Oh, God, wisdom, wisdom, wisdom. Please, God, wisdom.'

These habits develop rhythm and consistency and simplicity around prayer. And I keep lists – on my phone, in my diary, wherever – of things that niggle. Like that we need a new printer cartridge and it's not in this month's budget. I write it down. Tell God. Cast the burden. And I keep asking myself: 'Have I prayed about this as much as I've talked about it?'

Because, maybe, if we're breathing in God deeply all day – submitting to him the small decisions and events that make up ordinary life – then it won't be too hard to say yes when he asks us to pray – breathe deeply in him – all night for the life of a baby girl.

Or the salvation of a nation.

Or a changed world.

Part 4

Sow it

Living brave in community - and the change that it brings

We scatter truth seeds,
Tenderly water. Wait. Pray.
Reap rich grace harvest.

14

Tea and Zanzibar

She tells her love while half asleep,
In the dark hours,
*   With half-words whispered low:*
As Earth stirs in her winter sleep
*   And puts out grass and flowers*
*   Despite the snow,*
*   Despite the falling snow.*

Robert Graves[1]

I am my lover's, and my lover is mine.

Song of Songs 6:3

Life is hard because of dragons and dirt. Maybe that's why marriage is hard. Because when two become one? You've got to beat off your own dragons and another's. You've got two people's dirt under one roof. But this collision of lives is also what makes marriage such a brilliant idea. Because you've got someone to help you face the dragons. Someone to shine a light on your heart and offer goodness and grace of their own.

In our tenth year of marriage, we find ourselves on an island off the east coast of Africa. Close to the equator, and each other. They call Zanzibar the spice island. Perfect, yes, for celebrating ten years of spice? Ten years of decision-making and love-making. Home-making and baby-making. Mistake-making and dream-making.

The island is an eclectic mix of heat and dirt and poverty and luxury and energy and intoxicating beauty. There are barefoot locals with smartphones and bicycles. There are coral reefs and palm trees. There are bananas cooked in coconut milk. There's watermelon and bliss.

When I'm stressed? I speed up. When Murray is stressed ... he slows down. Which always makes getting to the airport boarding gate interesting. But here on the bright white soft sand, we hold hands and find again the common, comfortable pace of together. We walk for hours. Swim. Sleep. My stomach burns red because I haven't worn a bikini in six months. We find beach hotels for dinners and somehow stretch our dollars. We drink Kilimanjaro tea. We miss the boys. We talk.

We talk with gratitude about the rare mercy – the rich legacy – of growing up in happy homes. We talk about how the truth and courage on which our parents have built their marriages have bolstered our own.

1. Graves, R., 'She tells her love while half asleep', in *Inscapes: A collection of relevant verse* compiled by Malan, R. (Cape Town: Oxford University Press, 1969), 186.

Like, the profound truth we've learned from the Reyburns is the importance of tea. The Reyburns are unabashed tea buffs. Don't give a Reyburn a bag in a mug. Oh no. It's teapots and cosies all the way. It's pouring the milk *first*. It's a refined process and a ritual and an occasion every time and it happens on average four times a day. But it's not really about the tea. It's about what happens when there's an intention to sit down and wrap hands around mugs and cease whatever is driving the day. It's about making time for relational connections in the everyday noise and mess of life. We've carried the habit that sustains the value into our own marriage. Tea – and unpacking the highs and lows of the day – is so often the thing I can't wait to get to because if we can just get to tea, I know that everything will be all right in the end. And as Sonny says in *The Best Exotic Marigold Hotel*, 'If it's not all right then it's not yet the end.'[2]

The wisdom we've taken from the Smiths is to look to the future. To plan wisely so that we keep in step with each other – emotionally, spiritually, financially, socially, intellectually. I remember my mom telling me when I was little how important it is in marriage to make mutual decisions so that as husband and wife you change and grow together, rather than changing and growing apart. She said I should take an interest in my husband's work and passions – and share mine with him – so that we would stay friends and allies. My parents have taught us well the practicalities of life – money and house-keeping and DIY – the surface things that, handled right, make for deep harmony.

It's this combined legacy – the importance of small everyday decisions that refresh the relationship, and the importance of big lifetime decisions that map out a future – that prompts us after three years of marriage to open a savings account called 'Tenth Anniversary'. Every month, or whenever we can manage it, we put away R50. Sometimes R200. Sometimes hope. We talk about going

---

2.   Parker, O., *The Best Exotic Marigold Hotel*, directed by John Madden (London: Blueprint Pictures, 2011).

back to Greece, or Victoria Falls, or Cape Town. We decide to celebrate somewhere neither of us has been – somewhere that will almost certainly involve adventure. Kind of like the future. So in the end, seven years of saving buys us three days in Zanzibar.

And it's perfect.

It's taken us eighty-four months to save up for celebrating ten years. And it's taken some courage to say no to the nag of school fees and renovations and other responsible grown-up things. But over those eighty-four months, we've had approximately 21 900 cups of tea. That's a lot of conversation. A lot of grappling with tough decisions. A lot of disagreeing. A lot of laughter. A lot of spilling tears of frustration or grief or PMS. A lot of love. And it's so exciting – so right – to chill to a standstill on a tropical island and revel in a decade of drinking all that tea.

We eat calamari and we talk about how some people have been critical of our getaway. We've had everything from, 'Why are you going for so *short*? You should totally go for at least two weeks!' to 'I could *never* leave my children for *three nights* …'. But we agree that sometimes we just have to have the courage to shut out the critics and trust God for the wisdom and discernment to make the right decisions for *our* marriage. Because no one else is part of our marriage. It's just us. And we're feeding our marriage. We're not feeding the sceptical bystanders. I say it often – to myself and to pregnant friends and to anyone who will listen – that if we give our kids nothing but a happy marriage, we've given them the greatest gift.

Still, it's been hard to put life on hold – even for three days – and to trust God to carry kids and calendars and ongoing commitments while we take time that feels selfish to find refuge to rejoice in our journey. But we do it. And really, we need to do it every day. We need to find a way to carry with us – into the normal of hectic humdrum life – this coconut shade and cardamom spice.

Kind of like Solomon did.

And I get that it's not everyone's cup of tea to compare the girl of your dreams to pomegranates and flocks of goats. But it was, three thousand years ago. Solomon's Song of Songs – the book sandwiched sexily between Ecclesiastes and Isaiah – is kind of freaky like that. Reams of ancient-Near-East erotica.

I love the poetry – poignant and down-to-earth and transcendent and gloriously romantic. But it's not just the poetry. There's a beautiful truth that recurs and it's this very thing – this thing of *refuge*.

The girl says, 'Take me with you; come, let's run! The king has brought me into his bedroom ... My lover is mine, and I am his.' The guy says, 'You are my private garden, my treasure, my bride, a secluded spring, a hidden fountain.'[3] Their passionate sense of belonging exclusively to each other creates a sensual sanctuary.

They're together.

Hidden.

Safe.

We see it back home and on Sky News and on this green patch of paradise in the sea: the world is a crazy, broken place. People hurt and hate. Landmines lurk. Even the sincerest intentions don't always shield us from being blown up on the road. It's war out there. And I'm not a pessimist. Just realistic. I shouldn't expect the world to be anything other than wrecked. That way, when I notice how by God's grace it is still shot through with devastating beauty, that beauty is all the more breathtaking.

But if lovers are to survive, thrive and *change* this world of war zones, we need a refuge.

When I started dating Murray, I knew he was different because when I was with him I felt wholly, inexplicably safe. It was like coming home from a long, rough, dirty journey – and then having a hot shower and walking barefoot on soft clean carpet and having tea

---

3. Song of Songs 1:4, 2:16, 4:12

in my own kitchen. That feeling, you know: Ah. At last. I'm home. I belong. I'm away from the dangers of the elements and the unknown.

I also knew he was different because the refuge I had found wasn't boring. It freed me. It was a safety that allowed me to become what I was born for. A world of adventure was unlocked. It was thrilling. We had Our Love Song, as you do. It was Bruce Springsteen's 'Born to run'. Murray would get a look in his eyes whenever it played and I was a goner.

> '... let me in, I wanna be your friend,
> I wanna guard your dreams and visions ...
> I gotta find out how it feels;
> I want to know if love is wild, girl, I want to know if love is real.
>
> ... I'll love you with all the madness in my soul;
> Someday, girl, I don't know when, we're gonna get to that place
> Where we really want to go and we'll walk in the sun ...
> baby, we were born to run ...'[4]

The truth is that marriage is a picture of how Christ loves the church.[5] We were born to run into the arms of Jesus, to find refuge in his forgiveness and to be set free to live his dreams for us. And on the journey towards marriage? Those travelling solo might ask: 'Am I the kind of refuge that a world-weary, true-love-longing traveller would be passionately relieved to discover?'

For me and Murray, the refuge of a Jesus-centred marriage means a forever commitment. It means no secrets, no deceit, no competition. It means knowing all the weird, human things about each other – like that I'll get a headache if the hotel mattress is dodgy and Murray will get sick on the boat if we go snorkelling off the reef – and circumnavigating those things with easy acceptance and humour. It means that he's the phlegmatic-melancholic *yes* to

---

4. Springsteen, B., 'Born to run', *Born to run*, © 1975, 2003 by ASCAP (Johannesburg: Sony BMG Music Entertainment Africa (Pty) Ltd).
5. Ephesians 5:21–33

my sanguine-choleric. My friend Debbie says, 'Stop waiting for your husband to be perfect. Just enjoy him.' That's refuge.

And refuge is trust and forgiveness and understanding and win-win. It's being fed and clothed, rested and restored – physically, emotionally, intellectually, spiritually. It's a haven for gathering body and soul together, and for regaining passion and perspective. It's the freedom to tease each other mercilessly because we both know that the teasing is just light loving, not pointed scorn. It's shelter from storms and assailants. It's private peace when the world is falling apart. It's unedited, unadulterated fun.

But to live into all this truth – to build a refuge – takes the constant courage of daily decisions to do the Next Right Thing.

And the next right thing might be to pack your best bikini for the beach.

It might be to put the kettle on one more time.

15

Borrowed

Remember how the Psalmist described children? He said that they were as an heritage from the Lord, and that every man should be happy who had his quiver full of them. And what is a quiver full of but arrows? And what are arrows for but to shoot? So, with the strong arms of prayer, draw the bowstring back and let the arrows fly – all of them, straight at the Enemy's hosts.

Jim Elliot, in a letter to his parents[1]

For this child I prayed; and the Lord has given me my petition which I asked of him ...

1 Samuel 1:27

I didn't really want to be a mom.

I was terrified that if I had kids, they might not like me. And I was terrified that I would damage them by repeating the mistakes of moms through the ages or making new – worse – mistakes in trying to avoid the old ones. I didn't know how *not* to project my insecurities and biases. Plus, I made babies cry and I didn't know what to say to anyone under the age of twelve. I always thought that having kids was the right thing to do – kind of. Like deworming your pets and paying traffic fines. But I had no desire to peer broodily into anyone else's pram. Like, ever.

Then one day a counsellor told me that all those things were true. She said that every parent damages their kid. Every parent tries so hard not to make the mistakes of their own parents that they make fresh mistakes of their own. She wasn't a fatalist. She was encouraging me to accept the inevitable and live *anyway* – live bravely – into whatever my future held.

And I'm living it. Because I'm pretty sure there are days my kids don't like me. I have definitely hurt them. Overcompensated. Allowed my junk to rub off on them. Some days my words are too heavy. Some days I make them cry.

But the truth is that something much bigger and more significant than all that happened when my body produced two humans. Something glorious. Something jaw-droppingly powerful. Something that dispelled the fear and washed up courage.

I've said in the acknowledgements of this book that my sons broke open my heart and I found an abyss of love that must have been there all along. The ground gave way before me and I didn't know I was capable of diving into such depths of compassion. Things that used to be super important to me suddenly weren't. And new things became paramount.

---

1.   Quoted in Rainey, D. and B., *Moments with you: Daily connections for couples* (Ventura: Regal Books, 2007).

I remember when they wheeled Cameron in for his first cataract surgery. The theatre doors closed and I wept like my soul had snapped. Because my hope had been wheeled into that theatre and I didn't know if it would come out whole.

And I remember my first day home from the hospital with Scott. Cozied up and nursing my baby son. I would be on maternity leave for the next four months. I was passionate about St Alban's College and the boys I taught there. But I remember thinking that if someone called to tell me that the school had burned down, I may well have looked up, gone, 'Oh,' and carried on allowing the world to be eclipsed by the magnificence of ten tiny perfect toes.

Having kids plays out differently for different people. For me, it was euphoric. Whole parts of me came wondrously alive.

But having kids forced me to confront hard truth. I had to be excruciatingly honest with myself about my failures and shortcomings. While parenthood ushered in startling love, I also saw sides of myself – ugly, angry, caustic sides – that had never before had cause to surface.

Like, when our boys were younger, their whining would wear me down something desperate. A relentless erosion of my endurance. Every means of discipline I tried seemed to make things worse. One day I picked them up from preschool after a day of teaching. All the way home, Cam whined and moaned and threw sulky tantrums on the backseat. I reached the end of myself. Screeched into the driveway. Slammed my car door. Burst into the house leaving the boys strapped in their seats so that they wouldn't see the tantrum I was about to throw. I flung my laptop on the floor. It was in its carry bag, but I flung it hard. Screamed and cried and wracked out sobs to God about *why why why* wasn't he *helping* me? And why was this all so bloody *hard?*

The chip off the corner of the laptop keyboard reminded me for a long time of my fallibility. And I realised that parenthood – the long process of instilling truth and calling out courageous obedience – demanded truth, courage and obedience from me like nothing I'd ever come up against.

It's difficult to model for my boys what it looks like to handle external life pressures and internal heart entanglements. I'm humbled every time I confess to them that I have cockroaches in my heart and need their forgiveness. And parenting can totally overwhelm me. A lot of the time I don't know what I'm doing. I have to react so fast that there isn't even time for a gut feeling to develop.

And yet, every morning, my boys patter down the passage with bed hair and sleepy eyes and so much grace for me. They're so pleased to see me. And I think how for as long as my Heavenly Father is not giving up on parenting me, I will not give up on parenting them. I hang on to the hope that each new, different day will bring new mercies,[2] and that each new, different day will find us different too. My boys will be different: bigger, cleverer, more handsome. And I will be different: more and more dependent on grace.

On the incredible days and on the disastrous days of being a parent, it's a relief to know the truth that my sons are God's before they are mine and that they will be his for eternity. It's a relief to know that I am not wholly responsible for them. I don't need to figure out their futures on my own. As much as God is lending them breath, he is lending them to me – flesh of my flesh – closer than breathing – yet his handiwork.

So I'm acutely aware that I am holding their hearts in borrowed time. They are my greatest long-term offshore investments. I'm trusting for dividends in eternity. I'm hoping for a harvest in their own grown-up families one day when they walk free from what we've planted under this roof.

---

2. Lamentations 3:23

The flipside of this truth about borrowed time is that as parents we're working against the clock. We have so much to teach them. So much truth to translate into their widening realities. And only so much time. Every sunset closes off another small chunk of life to love and guide and influence them for God's purposes.

Which can paralyse me just a bit.

Because, as Sandra Stanley says, the days feel long but the years are so short.[3] And the pressure of parenting well in what will end up as a split second of life has me second-guessing what I'm investing in the hours that drag towards bedtime because the day has me frazzled. I find myself asking, 'Will my rebukes make them feel rejected? What nasty memory am I making? Am I being too much the proverbial *good* mom – the one who does everything for her kids – instead of the *great* mom I want to be – the one who gives them the gift of independence and confidence and the satisfaction of a job well done?'

What frees me on the doubtful days is the truth that God has drawn the timelines around my season of motherhood. And in the past, present or future there's never been a mom like me. Or like you. I am freed by the truth that I am not my mom, or my mom-in-law, or my sisters, or any one of my mom friends who seem to be winning at this thing and always have great hair days. I learn heaps from all of these women. I see my blind spots in the mirror of their strengths. But God isn't calling me to *be* them. And he isn't calling them to be the mother of my sons. That job description fits only me. I am freed by the truth that, as someone has said, I can give my children the gift of my strengths and trust God to tweak my course when I bend to my weaknesses. I can trust him to convict me – to temper my faults and flaws – when I try to plot my own way.

***

3.   Stanley, A. and S., *Future Family*, DVD (Alpharetta: North Point Resources, 2012).

Carmine Gallo says that creativity thrives under constraints.[4] I think the same is true of courage. There are time constraints around being a parent. And money constraints and knowledge constraints and general life constraints. And yet feeling cornered can be our call to action. The constraints needn't make us less effective. They can be the very thing to electrify our influence. Maybe – to be creative, courageous moms and dads – we need to harness the energy generated by the constraints and channel it into a radical commitment to pray and obey.

Early in 2014, I wrote *The Prayer Manifesto for Moms* (and if you email me, I'll send it to you for free). I wrote these prayers – one for each day of the month – not because I had it all together and knew just how to pray for my kids. I wrote them out of a keen awareness that I cannot – *cannot* – mother on my own. I need daily assurance that my children and I are in the hands of a great God who longs to fulfil what he has stitched into our DNA, for our good and his glory.

I'm learning to pray through the day – as they're riding bikes or rescuing beetles. And I'm trusting God to put thoughts in my head and instincts in my gut concerning my children.

Even when the intuitions don't make sense.

Like, it's just past 7 p.m. – at *last*. Stories have been read. Teeth brushed. Prayers. Kisses. Love yous. Love you toos. Nighty-night.

And my promise:

'I'll come check on you now-now, OK? Just making tea.'

I do about three million things fast because at last I'm hands-free, then I head for the kitchen where there's fudge and Murray and *tea* and grown-up tell-me-your-day conversation. I'm down the passage and I hear it –

Go back.

Oh.

You promised.

---

4. Gallo, C., *Talk like TED* (New York: St. Martin's Press, 2014), 149.

And again – Still Small Voice –
Obey.
Sigh. I did say I'd check on them. *Surely* they're asleep?
Go back.

I turn. Tiptoe into the gloom of their ABC-Gruffalo-Pooh-Bear-world-map-solar-system room. Cam breathes slow. All run out of fun and resting deep. But Scott – blonde curls restless on his pillow – big eyes peering solemn above the duvet –

'Mom please you snuggle wif me?'

Something solid in me oozes soft. 'Sure, darling.'

We snuggle. He clutches tight round my neck and declares truth for us both – to comfort and convince –

'There are no monsters under my bed.'

'No, none!' I agree earnestly. 'No monsters.'

'I yuv you so much Mom.'

The kettle whistles and the tea can wait. I'm lying with my boy because the morning will come soon enough to consign another night to the past, and now, while he still needs me, I'm praying that I'll keep obeying so he'll keep remembering that I'll keep coming back.

Parenthood is more than a relentless refereeing of right from wrong. It's holding small hands through these borrowed days and trusting for wisdom to step in the direction of life and grace, because a discipled life *is* a disciplined life.

And when I'm not sure of the next step? I pause and think about the kind of men I hope will be waiting at the end of the aisle one day for the daughters-in-law that I trust are in our future. The kind of men that I hope will walk into interviews and wow whatever panels God puts before them with quiet, remarkable, unpretentious confidence in their skills and in the God who bestowed them.

Sometimes the next step is letting go of their hands just a little

– to show them that they are responsible for their lives. To show them that they dare not develop a victim mind-set – as if the world owes them something. To show them that life experience doesn't buy wisdom – *evaluated* life experience buys wisdom.

Sometimes the next step is setting them up for success – like, putting the tomato sauce on the lowest shelf in the fridge so that they can set the table and know that small brave helpers add value to this family.

Sometimes the next step is choosing words carefully. I try hard to lay off the sarcasm. And we try to speak a love language that balances grace and holiness. We don't talk about *punishment* when they've been dishonest, disrespectful or disobedient. Because Jesus took all our punishment on the cross. We talk about *consequence*. And helping them to *remember* not to do this again. And how *sorry* we are that they've sinned – the way God is grieved by sin and broken relationships. Always, we offer forgiveness.

I'm praying – for you and me, friend – that we would know when and how to protect our children from external forces that seek to destroy them. And that we would know when to let the external forces take their course to shape character.

I'm praying that we would call out of them the courage to clean out their hearts.

I'm praying that we would discipline, train and coach our kids in this blink of borrowed time, so that one day we can befriend them.

I'm praying that we would live our stories brave, and inspire our children to do the same.

I'm praying that we wouldn't clutch our children too tightly but that we would carry them carefully, in awe of the wonder of them, until they can carry themselves –

And change the world.

16

Soft steel

We all mold one another's dreams. We all hold each other's fragile hopes in our hands.

Anonymous

Your love for one another will prove to the world that you are my disciples.

John 13:35

It's Thursday night. I'm doing my best to get the boys into bed before our cell group arrives at sevenish because I know if they're still awake when Eric comes, it'll be another fifteen minutes before their excitement is lowered to a level compatible with sleep. Beds are ready in the playroom for the van Reenen kids. They bypass the kitchen – choose books – lie quiet like this is home. The Hewitt girls find blankets and lay claim to the sleeper couch in the study, or pass out on Ena's lap so that the soundtrack to our discussion is delicate snoring.

We've been hosting this group in our home for eight years. Bible study, home group, life group, care group – call it what you will. We laugh a lot, eat a lot, argue Apple versus Android, election versus free will, pray, laugh some more.

We're a mix. On the spectrum of Calvinist to Catholic to occasional charismatic, we've pretty much got everyone covered. We represent three local churches, which is unusual but it works just fine for us. Just fine for this small segment of the body. We're a fusion of different passions and personalities, callings and careers. Strong temperaments that don't water down opinion for the sake of another's ego. And yet there's deep love. Acceptance and genuine giving a damn. We do life together – kids and food, stress and joy. We celebrate promotions and sympathise over setbacks. We mark births, deaths and adoptions. We've cried together and fallen asleep on the couches together because Thursday nights sometimes come at the end of long weeks. We build rest into our community – meet for six weeks, rest for the seventh – and we rest on what Augustine said: 'In essentials unity. In non-essentials liberty. In all things love.' [1]

Our cell group is a microcosm of most communities – churches, families, schools, organisations and nations. We go through sweet spots and sludgy hard-going spots. Some Thursdays I look forward to it all day and some Thursdays I'd love a night off.

1. Attributed to Augustine of Hippo, 354–430 AD

But the truth is that communities keep going – keep growing – if you have the courage to keep building with soft steel.

It takes courage to be soft.

Hard hearts are easy to keep. And they keep others out. Hard hearts scoff that soft hearts are pathetic. Weak. Soft in the head.

But the hard hearts have it wrong. Because it takes the marvellous strength of the brave to be soft. It takes courage to live the truth that *not* loving people is not an option for Jesus followers. His love for us compels us to keep a soft heart and open doors to people in our lives and communities. On Thursday nights and every other day or night of the week, I need to be in a soft place to receive people, whether they arrive with sharp edges or whether they arrive with no edges and need to be held together.

And it takes courage to be steel.

Flaking out on others is the easy default. Facebook lets us opt out with a *maybe*. Because the truth is that we've become insular and individualistic. Social media makes for mass instant connections that are vast and shallow. Virtual associations are vague. It costs me nothing to hit 'like' on someone's post because I don't have to leverage my time or my resources – who I am – for the sake of someone else and their best interests. I can get away with not loving them. And while I may or may not be held accountable for knowing what's trending on Twitter, I will for sure be held accountable for how I treated the people who filled my days.

It takes courage to be steel because people's arms get heavy and you may need to hold them up for weeks – years – a lifetime.[2] You may need to be the steel that reinforces the faith of those God has given you to love. And sometimes you need to steel yourself against judgements and passing remarks because the people in your community? They're not perfect, and neither are you.

---

2. Exodus 17:11–13

Being soft steel to others – being brave enough to say *yes* to community – means learning how to navigate people with wisdom, discernment and sensitivity. When do I give space? When do I hold close? Because community is all about translating our intentions into someone else's reality.

When we realised our baby boy was blind, Murray was broken. He didn't want cheer-up-God's-in-control verses. He didn't want to hear what a privilege it was to be chosen for this trial. A lot of our friends avoided him because they didn't know how to penetrate his anger and grief. And he'll never forget what it meant to him when his friend, Andries, arrived at his practice in the middle of a work day and said, 'I don't know what to say. I don't have words. But I'm just praying so much for you.' And when his friend, Paul, took him for breakfast and said, 'Me too. I know about being angry at God. I don't have answers but I'm with you and I'm praying.' Like Job's friends (before they totally messed up with stupid advice), they just sat silent with him in the dust.[3] The power of that kind of soft-steel community? No words.

And sometimes, being soft steel to others means being brave enough to say *no* to community. Because a community can gather velocity and momentum and you can be swept up by the vision and the compulsion to. Do. Everything.

Except that Jesus didn't do everything. He didn't heal everyone. He didn't preach everywhere. He did the work of each day and he did it well. And we would do well not to try to fill all the gaps that need filling in a community. We would do well to do the work that we are uniquely called to do because less really is more. A few things done well are always better than a dozen things slapped hit-or-miss together. We're not supposed to be able to do everything or

---

3. Job 2:13

146

be involved everywhere. We're created with gaps, too, and there's something beautiful about giving those around us the space and freedom to use their gifts to fill us.

Jesus taught his friends about community when he had supper with them for the last time. Judas has left the room to split on the Son of God. Jesus knows. Death is near. He's about to enter his glory – about to leave them –
This is it.
He looks with love around the table – gives his parting instruction:

> 'So now I am giving you a new commandment: Love each other. Just as I have loved you, you should love each other. *Your love for one another will prove to the world that you are my disciples.*' [4]

His parting command isn't, 'Memorise Scripture to prove to the world that you are my disciples.' Though I'm a huge fan of that practice. He doesn't say, 'Build houses for Habitat for Humanity to prove to the world that you are my disciples.' Though that is life-or-death crucial. He doesn't say, 'Make sure everyone agrees on the doctrines of baptism, predestination and homosexuality in the church to prove to the world that you are my disciples.' Though I'm clear and pretty immovable on all those things. He says, 'Love each other. Just as I have loved you, you should love each other.'
Of course, prioritising love doesn't mean compromising beliefs. Jesus never did that. He was hard core. Resolved. He never sidestepped the truth to placate or fit in. He wasn't scared of pointing to the ideal – though he knew how this would offend – he was *steel*. Yet he didn't condemn those who fell short of it – he was *soft*. Community love means you keep going back to the pages of

---

4.   John 13:34–35, (emphasis mine)

Scripture – together – to wrestle with raw, difficult truth – to thrash out theology and lean into grace and truth in this post-postmodern culture of anything goes because, 'by this everyone will know that you are my disciples, if you love one another.'[5]

There's no escaping the design of creation. We're made for relationships. It's kind of obvious because God keeps making more and more people and putting them all on this one small planet. It's like he's saying, 'This isn't crowded. This is community.'

To which our culture says, 'Sorry, but I don't have *time* for community.'

And yes, the bad news is that people are *busy*. But the good news is that people have *choices*. We can decide to link into a community. We can decide to spend the energy and intention it takes to forge relationships that are close, deep and strong.

It takes courage to be in community – to trust God to order our private worlds and to bring across the tidy lines and the blank margins of each day whomever he chooses. And as he does that, maybe we should ask these kinds of questions:

Who did God add into the mix of my day?

As far as it depended on me, was there life in the connections?

Was I the 'yes' to someone's question, 'Is Jesus for real?'

Was I soft steel?

Because a good day isn't about measurable achievements or what got ticked off the list. It's about attitudes and actions and how they affected the warm bodies around us. Maybe we need to bring this kind of community to dinner parties and school car parks and prayer groups and WhatsApp chats because –

By this everyone will know that we are his disciples.

And by this, we might just change the world.

---

5.   John 13:35, New International Version

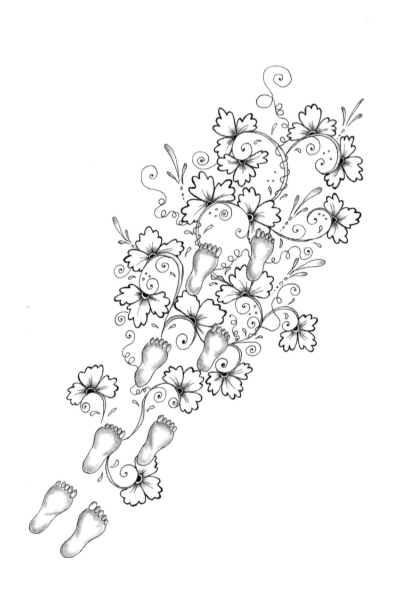

17

Feet

What lies behind us and what lies before us are small matters compared to what lies within us.

Ralph Waldo Emerson[1]

Mighty hero, the Lord is with you! ...
Go with the strength you have ...

Judges 6:12, 14

I've got gross feet. Really. I only have eight-and-a-half toenails, for starters. True story. (Long story.) And my feet just aren't delicate or pretty. I had a boyfriend once who thought it would be funny to quote Psalm 139 at me: 'Dee, you're fearfully and wonderfully made. But your feet – they're just fearfully made.'

But I've come to love my feet. Because they're the feet God chose to make for me, and because they've taken me to streets and beaches and mountaintops on almost every continent, and because they keep me humble. A big head gives me a better view of my feet so when I get proud it just takes a glimpse of those toenails for my head to shrink back to an appropriate size.

And I've thought about my feet a lot as they relate to leadership.

Anyone who wants to change the world is a leader so I guess I am. And, for sure, you are too. Moms and dads are leaders. Small people look to us. Teachers and architects and entrepreneurs and physiotherapists and gardeners and accountants and friends are leaders. Anyone who is passionate about maximising time and potential and leveraging influence for the Kingdom is a leader.

And if you're convinced that you're so *not* a leader? You're leading a life. That makes you a leader. All your days you'll be putting one foot in front of the other. And if you do that well – if your life is a lavish expenditure of your time and your potential within the context that God has set you – you may look back and find a bunch of people following you.

Every truth about leadership demands that you be brave because the soul of leadership is courage and there's no space for cowardice. It takes courage to lead because leaders are initiators and early adopters. Leading requires walking out front. Stubbing toes on obstacles misjudged or unexpected because we're the first to get to them.

---

1.   Emerson, R.W., *The Essential Writing of Ralph Waldo Emerson*, ed. Brooks, A. (New York: Classic Books International, 2010).

And it takes courage to lead because leaders are lonely. Once when I shared with my sister, Coralie, how I felt on the fringes everywhere and at the centre nowhere, she said to me, 'But God has *placed* you.'

She reminded me that God is sovereign over secularism. He has the ability to put us where he wants us, regardless of whether or not it makes sense to us or to others. And it got me thinking about Joseph's life as it unfolded after his technicolour dreamcoat got him into trouble with his brothers.[2]

Joseph was lonely. In the top strata of Egyptian aristocracy, and in prison, he didn't fit in. His intentions were misunderstood.

Yet Joseph was promoted. God chose his position. He didn't have the right qualifications by any stretch of the CV. But, like Jesus, he 'left his case in the hands of God, who always judges fairly.'[3]

And so Joseph was used. Mightily. Reverberations resounding in eternity. And I'm all goose-bumps and gratitude when I think how we serve the same God that Joseph served. The God of eternity and every day. The God who split the Red Sea and can write your résumé and protect your reputation.

Because whether you're a big-shot leader or a hardly-noticed leader, you can be lonely – in any organisation or community or family. You're in front – on the edge – plotting a course – launching – deciding – sticking with it. And people are quick to hang back and leave you exposed. (Haven't I done that to people whom I've said I would follow?) Other times, leaders do enjoy a following – but little fellowship.

But there's strength and keep-on-keeping-on confidence in knowing that God is your promoter in career and community, friendships and family. Corporate steps and closed circles are nothing to him. He will put you where he wants you. For your good and for his glory. You needn't shoulder-rub or name-drop or trumpet-blow to find out or fit in. Just be faithful. Just keep giving your very best you to the circumstances in

---

2. Genesis 37–50
3. 1 Peter 2:23

which you find yourself. Even when affirmation dries up and doubt drenches the trenches of your mind, don't get tired of doing good. The harvest is quietly ripening. In due course, you'll reap.[4]

Because being a successful leader, really, is just putting one foot in front of the other. Left. Right. Left. Right. Love. Righteousness. Love. Righteousness.

I remember standing barefoot at the stove at the beginning of a year in which I faced a new and daunting leadership challenge. I felt that there were critical eyes on me. People watching and wondering and waiting for me to fail. I kept stirring through the steam and I felt God say to me that day that he would *protect, establish* and *promote* me. Those three words became my mainstay on tough days and they energised me to lead boldly and without fear of recrimination. All that time I had a sense of God encircling me. I was protected. My feet were on the rock. I was established. And he had the power and wisdom to hide me or display me as it seemed good to him.

Another fact about feet? They're made of clay.

Like the feet of the statue in Nebuchadnezzar's dream,[5] they spell destruction if we think we can do leadership alone. The moment we get proud and stop depending daily on Jesus for insight and guidance – the moment we stop cleaning out our hearts – our leadership becomes inefficient, ineffective and detrimental to those who are following.

The truth is, a leader needs feet that stand firm. She needs to know exactly where she's standing, and why. She needs to be comfortable with the idea of standing there for as long as it takes. And when it comes to stepping on toes – because, um, you will – a leader should take advice from Dr Seuss:

You have brains in your head.
You have feet in your shoes.

4. Galatians 6:9
5. Daniel 2

154

You can steer yourself
any direction you choose …
So be sure when you step.
Step with care and great tact
and remember that Life's
A Great Balancing Act.[6]

So as leaders, with feet, we need to stand on our own. And wash another's.

That's how Jesus led. He lived and breathed and died for truth. He displayed the courage of unthinkable compassion. He simultaneously held together the atoms of all creation while stooping low to wash filth from feet. Mighty hero. Humble servant.

In the upper room with his disciples – death drawing near – Jesus gives us this astounding and ultimate lesson on leadership:

> Jesus knew that the Father had given him authority over
> everything and that he had come from God and would return
> to God. So he got up from the table, took off his robe, wrapped
> a towel around his waist, and poured water into a basin. Then
> he began to wash the disciples' feet, drying them with the towel
> he had around him.[7]

So Jesus has just come to the realisation – again – that all. Power. Is. His. In and above and beyond the universe. And the very next thing he does? He gets up and washes feet. He says that same night – God with skin on: 'For I am among you as one who serves.'[8]

The Kingdom of God is always the crazy beautiful upside-down opposite to what the world is yelling about power and pre-eminence. And as leaders, in whatever Kingdom capacity, the more power we have, the more we should be serving.

Because that kind of leadership? It might just change the world.

6. Dr. Seuss, *Oh, the places you'll go* (New York: Random House Inc., 1957), 2, 40.
7. John 13:3–5
8. Luke 22:27

Epilogue

Rock it

A letter to my sons about living fully - and the courage it requires

There are far, far better things ahead than any we leave behind.

C.S. Lewis[1]

So be truly glad. There is wonderful joy ahead ...

1 Peter 1:6

Dearest Cam and Scott

People who write books – and people who write books about people writing books – they talk a lot about platform. And by platform they mean the people who are going to buy your book. Followers. Friends. Fans. They mean the people who make you feel famous.

But really, you are my platform. You watch me every day. You see me 'constantly risking absurdity' – trying to make art with my life. And when I'm 'balancing on eyebeams / above a sea of faces'[2] – the eyes and the faces are really just yours. Your love suspends me.

So I'm writing this last chapter to you because, as your mom, I have a unique dispensation of authority in your lives (for now). And because my greatest success lies not in how many books I sell, but in how much truth and courage I pour into you. And because I'm desperate to teach you well how you only get one shot at this gig called life. You are my highest calling. And you make me feel famous.

I want to write to you about celebration. About how God is most glorified in us when we are most satisfied in him.[3]

I want to write to you about living fully.

You know me – how much I love to travel. Travel has always been kind of how I define *living fully*. Maybe it's because, really, I'm a lot bolder when I travel. The glorious sensory assault of being thrust from my comfort zone – from the rhythms and routines of normal – gives me big-picture freedom to live adventurously. So I've slept on a beach in Spain and on an airport floor in Tel Aviv and on a train platform in Berlin and on a bus through Morocco with vomit sloshing side to rock-reeling side under the seats. These are all great stories to tell (except maybe the one with the vomit) because I felt so *alive* when I was living them. I was pushed to look at the context and say, 'It is what

---

1.   Lewis, C.S., *Collected Letters* (Eugene: Harvest House Publishers, 1993).
2.   Ferlinghetti, L., 'Constantly risking absurdity', in *Inscapes: A collection of relevant verse* compiled by Malan, R. (Cape Town: Oxford University Press, 1969), 116.
3.   Piper, J., *Don't waste your life* (Wheaton: Crossway Books, 2003), 28.

it is.' And then use the time available and the potential of the situation to make the best possible memory.

But the fact is that travel isn't just about TripAdvisor and passports and plane tickets and foreign streets. We're travelling all the time. We're all travelling through time, all together. All the sunrises it takes us to get from birth to death.

And we can make that same choice, in every context.

We can decide on the best possible memory.

We can decide to live fully.

You totally have to watch the movie *About Time*. It stars Bill Nighy and Rachel McAdams and it will probably change your life. I won't ruin it – but basically some of the characters get the chance to live a moment – a day – a whole season – over. Better. And they end up seeing that really, they only need to live it once. Because they always have the chance to decide first time around how they want a moment – a day – a whole season – to play out.

Because – did I mention this? – you can decide on the best possible memory. You can decide to live fully.

But boys, the reality is that the *full* life is the *alive* life and alive things keep growing and changing so the truth about living fully is that you need to keep on applying all these things – all the things I've written about in this book – when it's easy and obvious and when you fail and forget and when there's challenge and change.

There will always be dragons.

There will always be dirt.

Slaying the former and scrubbing out the latter has to be your habit, all your days.

The truth is that the *full* life is the *savoured* life. Big dreams grow slowly. Like big trees. They give shade for generations. Be patient. You can't hurry God. He's never late. Life is short, sure. But life is also long. There's time.

The truth is that the *full* life is the *surging* life. It's the bristling teeming bursting life. And the courage it demands is to hold that tension. Savour it. Let it surge. Don't try to escape time but rather keep pace with time and live it wild. Don't waste a moment. Fill up your days. Earn your years. Dig deep and live loud.

And leave the planet better than you found it. Seriously. This is a real possibility.

Because you've been created with passions and gifts to be used for good and if you know what they are, if you know yourself, and if you have the courage to own your potential, then you hold the key to the full life. I pray that you will see the truth about yourselves and have the courage to live out what God has put inside you, in obedience to his calling.

And if you can't quite figure out your passion and potential? Steve Jobs would have asked you, 'What makes your heart sing?'[4] What energises you and flips your stomach? What are you excited about before you do it, while you're doing it, and when you think about it afterwards? What do you do that makes people go, 'Oh, look, he's in his *element!*'

Sir Ken Robinson describes being in your element as the space where aptitude and passion collide.[5] Like, I love playing squash. I find it really fun. I suck at it. When I'm playing squash, I am not in my element. I'm pretty good at proofreading documents. It's mind-numbingly tedious. So when I'm proofreading, I'm not in my element. You might be good at something but it doesn't necessarily light your fire. You might really enjoy something but have scant talent for it. Neither scenario finds you in your element. Eric Liddell (the guy in *Chariots of Fire* who wouldn't compete on a Sunday) said, 'God made me fast, and when I run I feel his pleasure.'[6] When Eric

4. Gallo, C., *Talk like TED* (New York: St. Martin's Press, 2014), 22.
5. Robinson, K., *The Element: How Finding Your Passion Changes Everything* (New York: Penguin Group, 2009), 8.
6. Welland, C., *Chariots of Fire*, directed by Hugh Hudson (London: 20th Century Fox, 1981).

Liddell ran, he was in his element. Physically, emotionally, spiritually, intellectually.

And yet more important even than finding your sweet spot is deciding what you really want to give to this world. Not what you want out of life, but how you want to contribute. So that you can say with Tennyson, 'How dull it is to pause, to make an end, to rust unburnish'd, not to shine in use!'[7]

So, sons of mine, what do you love being good at and what gift do you want to give to the world?

Because I believe with the psalmist that God saw your unformed substance. That he knew the number of your days before the first one dawned.[8] That despite your (and everyone's) congenital sin defect, he crammed your DNA with uniqueness and latent possibility – astonishing capacities to be freed by Jesus' blood – so that you could be all he created you to be – all you already are in him. I'm passionate about raising you to be authentically resolved to live out the God-dreams woven in the darkness. Because 'God has plans which mortals don't understand. He rests in the womb when the new baby forms. Whispers the life dream to infinitesimal cells.'[9]

Finally, the truth is that it takes courage to live fully. It takes courage to celebrate in a dark world where there is most often more reason *not* to celebrate. But when you stop looking for answers in the mess – when you look up – when you boldly declare that there is hope in the grace and goodness of the living God in this life and the next, you will spread the light and the scent of him wherever you go. Celebrate, my loves. Sing. Turn the truth up loud and rock it. God inhabits the praises of his people.[10] The world will be different if your lives declare his greatness.

I have a friend whose son has a genetic degenerative condition

---

7. Tennyson, Lord Alfred, 'Ulysses', in *Inscapes: A collection of relevant verse* compiled by Malan, R. (Cape Town: Oxford University Press, 1969), 45.
8. Psalm 139:16
9. Attributed to Ellease Southerland (b. 1943).
10. Psalm 22:3

with a sinister prognosis. She says she feels as if she's travelling on Sani Pass. It's treacherous. Steep. Slippery. She can't see what's coming round the next corner. But she says that she would rather be on Sani Pass, where the view is spectacular and she's learning to drive really well, than on the easy flats of the Free State. She says she has reason to celebrate – that she wouldn't swap her journey for anything – because there is breathtaking beauty that can only be glimpsed by those with the courage to ride dangerous, difficult roads.

Anne Frank was thirteen years old when she and her family went into hiding. They were Jewish and it was 1942 in Nazi-occupied Amsterdam. During the two very quiet, very scary years that they spent holed up in a few square metres of hidden room, Anne displayed remarkable strength and resilience. The way she lived her life in those years – revealed through her diary after the war – changed the way people thought about hope and our ability to transcend horrifying circumstances. In a situation where she couldn't physically do very much at all, she did everything she could, and she was a world changer in her own right. She scrawled on her secret pages, 'How wonderful it is that nobody need wait a single moment before beginning to improve the world.'[11]

My little travellers through time, 'the Lord has told you what is good, and this is what he requires of you: to do what is right, to love mercy, and to walk humbly with your God.'[12]

How I celebrate over you.

And I know – like how a mom just knows because she *knows* – that you will change the world.

All my love always
Mom
xx

---

11. Frank, A., *The diary of a young girl* (Amsterdam: Contact, 1947).
12. Micah 6:8

Acknowledgements

To Murray – lover and friend. You are my refuge from a crazy world. You changed the colour of my life. Thank you for protecting me and for giving me the freedom to dream. Thank you for making sure that there was always tea, fudge and all the episodes of NCIS, ever. Thank you for reminding me not to panic. Thank you for your gentleness and generosity, your hugs, hilariousness and general awesomeness. You are my favourite forever.

To Cameron and Scott. You broke open Mommy's heart and I found an abyss of love that must have been there all the time. Thank you, thank you, thank you. My arms aren't strong enough and a lifetime isn't long enough to hug into you how much I love you.

To my parents, Deryck and Margie Smith. You have faithfully, lovingly and enthusiastically supported my big and little dreams, all my years. Thank you so very much. I love you.

To my parents-in-law, Lindsay and Yvonne Reyburn. Thank you for your immense love, and for the kindness, wisdom and generosity you bring to our lives.

To Christelle de Vries. Thank you for hearing my heart for each person who reads this book and for translating that into astounding beauty. I am so very glad to call you friend and to have shared this journey with you.

To Lisa-Jo Baker. Thank you for encouraging me to be obedient, one hot December night in Africa. Thank you for cheering me on from your side of the equator and thank you, friend, for the foreword of this book.

To Susan Prozesky. Gentle friend. Merciless editor. I wouldn't have wanted my book baby to fall into the hands of anyone but you. Thank you for your honesty, insight, scrutiny and advice, for the hours you invested in this book, and for keeping me more-or-less calm.

To Coralie van Reenen. Thank you for knowing all the bits of me and for loving me prayerfully through the writing of this book, with so much stability, acceptance and wisdom.

To Samantha-Leigh Bester and Shirley Stokker. Thank you for being my safe place. Thank you for your sincere excitement, for the time you sacrificed to talk things through with me, for knowing when to pray, and for believing in my dreams with unflagging enthusiasm. I treasure your friendship.

To Terry Brauer, Yolanda Collins, Debbie Holloway, Lourika Kotzee and Rebecca Le Roux. Thank you for your resolute commitment to pray for me for as long as it took me to do this thing. Thank you for honest feedback, indefatigable encouragement, faithful friendship and wild cheering. There is no way I could have written this book without you.

To Pam Ferreira. Thank you for seeing me. Thank you for making time to buy me breakfast once a month and for how much of yourself you have poured into me. God has used you in my life. *Seismically.* I will be grateful all my days, and then some.

To Brahm and Antoinette Hattingh. Thank you for loving me, praying for me and mentoring me for twenty-something years. Your wisdom, humility, easy grace and matter-of-fact holiness are so inspiring. I want to be like you when I'm big. Thank you for coming – quickly – the day I needed desperate prayer for this book.

To Brett 'Fish' Anderson and Bruce Collins. Living legends. Thank you for shouting my dream from the rooftops and for making me feel brave.

To Melanie de Kock and Shaleen Billson. I'm grateful and humbled to walk in the deep furrows that you have ploughed ahead of me. So much of who I am grew in our sisterhood. I love you so much.

To Ann Voskamp. Thank you for years of wisdom from a farm porch in Ontario. You have inspired me to be honest and vulnerable, so that others might be blessed. And I'm unspeakably grateful for the chance we had to connect in Atlanta.

To Jeff Goins. I feasted on everything you had to teach me about the craft. I devoured the inspiration you served up week after week. Thank you for convincing me that I really am a writer.

To Glenn Alexander, for your advice on social media marketing, and to Dave Strehler – friend and fellow writer – for your warmth and genuine support.

To my blog readers. Thank you for receiving with so much grace my weekly thoughts, and for believing I had something worth sharing.

To our cell group – the Bowies, Eberleins, Hewitts and van Reenens. To our church family and my Friday prayer group. You are my rhythm and my real. Thank you.

To the giants of the faith who don't know I exist but whose words have sunk solid in my soul. To the car-park moms who waved wild and warm and so often put the wind back in my sails. To others still who listened, challenged, inspired, supported, phoned, texted, tweeted, hugged, prayed and came over to play with my boys so I could get some writing done. You have shaped me, and I honour you.

And to Jesus Christ. King, Friend, Redeemer. Slayer of dragons. Cleanser of dirt. You are mighty to save. You make all the difference. Take your glory.